What Readers Are Saying about *Level Headed* ...

"This is not a rags-to-riches story, but more riches to rags to riches. It's a cautionary tale about how any good company can get off track if it strays from sound business principles. But this book shows that with the right team focusing on core values almost anything is possible."

> Dr. Joseph T. Wells, CFE, CPA
> Chairman of the Board of Directors
> Association of Certified Fraud Examiners

"An excellent example of the high value of servant leadership where senior leaders take care of the people, the people take care of the clients, the company takes care of the industry, and in doing so, increases profitability. The more we give the more we receive."

> Dr. William W. Badger
> Professor Emeritus, Del E. Webb School
> of Construction at Arizona State University.

"A wonderful example of the difference great leadership makes in creating value in a company." Sheryl Cefali

> Managing Director
> Duff & Phelps LLC

"Sundt walked its talk and is now reaping the benefits of strong leadership and committed teams. This company lives its core values and continually strives for excellence. They have made me a better consultant!"

> Bob Petrello
> President
> PRAXIS Leadership Systems

"A compelling 'inside' story about the courage and leadership needed to reinvent a company to meet current and future challenges—a must read for today's construction executive."

> David R. Lukens
> Chief Operating Officer
> Associated General Contractors of America

"A great story of how strong, decisive leadership, driven by data, can turn a company around. The clear statement of the problem, enrolling the leadership team and the call to action, which Doug led, saved Sundt."

> Tom Franz
> President /CEO of Greater Phoenix Leadership
> Intel Corporate Vice-President (retired)

"This is a book not only that small/medium company leaders and employees should read, but also leaders and managers at 501c3s, universities, and government. The need for focus, discipline, customer focus, and succession planning are critical to success and clearly illustrated in *Level Headed*. Accountability matters. A story well told and a job well done."

> Dr. William C. Harris
> President and CEO
> Science Foundation Arizona

"*Level Headed* is the fascinating narrative of a storied company led back from the edge of an abyss to best-in-class excellence by a pragmatic and visionary man. The evolution of Sundt during Doug Pruitt's leadership has been nothing short of remarkable. The lessons learned throughout this book are applicable to any business and provide a road map to success for both executives as well as young professionals. It's a must read."

> Susan Hecker
> Executive Vice President
> Gallagher Construction Services

"An amazing story of how great a company with a hundred years of incredible success, found itself on the brink of disaster and then, how dedicated, strong, new leadership, with a commitment to success, rescued the company and took it to even greater heights. All CEOs in the construction and infrastructure industry need to read this book."

> David F. Evans
> Founder and Chairman Emeritus
> David Evans and Associates, Inc.

"This is an amazing story about success. Every CEO needs to read this and I am sure, like me, they will see much of their own company in this book. It is so easy to lose focus in our companies and so hard to get it back. Doug and Richard faced it, solved it, and are sharing the results. This is a must read."

> Ted Aadland
> CEO of Aadland Evans Constructors
> President of Associated General Contractors 2010

"Leadership matters. The survival and subsequent success of Sundt is a testimony to the vision, leadership, and tenacity of Doug Pruitt. Making tough decisions and installing good management processes and systems kept Sundt from being another failure in a difficult industry. It is an uplifting and inspiring story."

> Hugh Rice
> Chairman of the Board Investment Banking
> FMI Corp.

"Very inspirational story of identifying corporate weaknesses, determining strategies to provide tactical solutions to overcome the issues that were preventing the company from becoming not just successful again, but an exemplary leader in the construction industry."

> Jerry Carlson
> President
> Carlson & Carlson, Inc.

What is this and how do I use it? It's called a QR code. It allows you to Get In the Loop with me! Use a barcode scanner on your smartphone to unlock special content, videos and rewards from the author. As you read, scan the QR content (updated periodically) throughout this book for an even deeper, richer experience of Level Headed.

Level Headed Videos

Asset Management

Business Development

Change and Innovation

ESOP

Gold Canyon Ranch

Strategic Management

Sundt Foundation

Technology

The Edge of the Abyss

Training and Development

Why The Book/Meet Authors

These videos may also be found on YouTube by searching for "Level Headed Sundt"

Level Headed

Inside the Walls of
One of the
Greatest Turnaround Stories
of the Twenty-First Century

Maintain discipline

Doug

J. Doug Pruitt and Richard Condit

Level Headed: Inside the Walls of One of the Greatest Turnaround Stories of the Twenty-First Century

Published by Wheatmark®
1760 East River Road, Suite 145, Tucson, Arizona 85718 U.S.A.
www.wheatmark.com

ISBN: 978-1-62787-108-2 (paperback)
ISBN: 978-1-62787-109-9 (ebook)

LCCN: 2014931969

DEDICATIONS

Richard

There are those who would argue that there are no longer enough heroes in the world. I would disagree as I think they are all around us, and while they may not get the notoriety of some more public figures, they are heroes nonetheless. I want to dedicate this book first to my hero, my wife, Paula. Her life's journey has been filled with courage, and I have been privileged to spend thirty-four years of my life with her. In the course of writing this book, Paula had a stroke and demonstrated amazing courage through that experience. I have been given a second chance at making sure she knows each and every day how much I love her and to express my good fortune at having her as my life partner. I love you, Paula.

Secondly, I want to dedicate this book to my co-author, Doug. Our personal and professional journey at times appears to be random, but I think there is a plan, or so it would seem in my case. It is very clear that Doug was the right person for Sundt at the right time, and I want to thank him for allowing me to be part of the team that turned around a company that was worth saving. Doug has been a good friend, an inspiration, a person who has provided me with the opportunity to be professionally challenged and has, because of his leadership, produced wealth for me and my family that has allowed us to do things that most educators can only dream of. Thank you, Doug!

Doug

I want to thank Becky, my wife and best friend for the past forty-four years, for her unwavering support and incredible advice and counseling during very difficult times. Her wisdom and insight was very instrumental in helping me see through the many problems we were struggling with and find the right solutions as we moved forward.

I also want to thank the many Sundt employee owners (some of whom are retired now) who didn't blink. They stood in there during difficult times and went the extra mile and did what needed to be done to right this ship and keep this company alive. We wouldn't be writing a book about this turnaround without their tremendous courage and loyalty.

All net proceeds of the sale of this book
go to the Sundt Foundation,
dedicated to children at risk.

Contents

INTRODUCTION

Staying level headed in business can often feel like trying to keep your balance in an earthquake. When you're trying to turn a business around from the brink of collapse, remaining level headed can be nearly impossible, yet it is a requirement for effective leadership and achieving consistently positive outcomes.

We use the words *I* and *we* a lot in this book because *we* are telling the story, but we are under no illusion that the two of us turned this company around by ourselves. It took a lot of people moving in the same direction and working hard so Sundt could survive. We wanted to honor those who fought alongside us these last thirteen years to save this wonderful company and the legacy of the Sundt family from extinction after more than one hundred years of business. In that way, we hope this book provides future leaders with the institutional memory of how we did it, and what things led to the decay so that they can avoid making the same mistakes.

We also want to provide you, the reader, with a fly-on-the-wall experience of what we were thinking, facing, and dealing with as we navigated the rocky road away from the edge of the abyss while trying to remain level headed through those turbulent times. This will give you some valuable insight into our decision-making process so you can garner insights into how to keep your own business thriving and how to find your way out of the inevitable pitfalls all companies face from time to time.

Lastly, we do not consider ourselves gurus or anything of the sort, but we have walked every step of the journey you are about to witness in the forthcoming pages, and have the scars, bruises, and success stories to prove it. We hope that by removing the veil and giving you an intimate and personal look into what we went through, you will find value for the time you have invested in reading this book.

We will share with you one of the most remarkable stories of a good company with a great reputation that got into serious financial trouble. Here was a revered, multigenerational family business, founded in 1890 by a Norwegian immigrant named M. M. Sundt with his box of handmade wooden tools in tow.

The company thrived for over a hundred years until suddenly, and seemingly without warning, it was headed toward a cliff. How could such a thing happen?

If you are in business, the answers will be familiar to you: lack of discipline, lack of focus, lack of organizational consistency, lack of employee training, poor succession planning, lack of investment in technology and education, and other familiar tunes sung by companies that fail (or come close to it). But Sundt *didn't* fail. In fact, we came back stronger than ever.

What can other businesses, especially in these troubled economic times, learn from our story and how we righted such a mighty ship again? Everything! We wouldn't be writing this book and sharing the story of Sundt's turnaround *for the very first time* if we didn't firmly believe this. That's right! In an age where the struggles and demises of corporate giants are very publicly broadcast all over cable media, we are sharing with you the story of one that slid under the headlines. If the story of Sundt were covered by the ravenous media, the headline would be: How Could Such a Good Company Get in Trouble so Quickly?

We appreciate your sincere interest in becoming a better leader—a level-headed one—and building (or rebuilding) a great company of your own.

Two Authors, One Great Story

The story of Sundt's near collapse and triumphant return from the edge of the abyss is packed with details and lessons that other businesses can learn from. It is also anchored in our respective, up-close, personal accounts of the incidents that led us down the road to trouble and how we recovered, ending up stronger than ever before.

While the two of us took on the task of writing this book, anyone who works in an organization understands that success and failure are a team sport. We will identify in these pages individuals who played key roles in making the turnaround at Sundt a success, but there are many others whom we have not mentioned. In the end it is the collective spirit of all the employee owners of Sundt who share in this great success story.

Another, perhaps unique, aspect of the two of us is that our professional experiences were very different before we worked together at Sundt. Doug had spent nearly twenty-five years at Sundt before Richard joined the company in 1993. Richard had spent almost twenty-three years in career and technical education as a teacher and state-level administrator. Neither of us signed on thinking that we would find ourselves faced with saving a sinking ship, but we had no choice.

Our unique blend of experiences and perspectives were helpful in addressing the serious problems we were facing and challenging each other's thoughts on the changes that needed to be made to save this company.

When such a story is being told by two separate voices with two unique perspectives of the events as they unfolded, the issue of a clear, consistent narrator voice comes into play. Our goal as writers was to maintain our individual voices when it came to sharing the intimate, fly-on-the-wall experiences while avoiding any confusion for you, the reader, as to which author is the narrator at which point.

To these ends we established the "default" narrator voice in the collective first person (*we, us, our*) as together, we guide you through the essential what, how, when, and why of this remarkable story. However, for those moments when, as individuals who lived these events on the front lines, we felt it imperative to share our candid, personal recollections, and observations, we distinguished the text clearly through specific formatting. We hope this results in a straightforward reading experience.

PROLOGUE: CAPTAIN OF A SINKING SHIP, 1992

Doug Pruitt, Chairman and CEO

"Bob is retiring and I've decided to make you president." The words were barely out of Wilson Sundt's mouth before he turned around and abruptly left my office. If what he had just said was not shocking enough, add to it that Wilson had driven two hours straight from Sundt's Tucson headquarters to my office in Phoenix to utter this one life-changing sentence! I jumped out of my chair and ran out of the building into the sweltering summer heat, chasing Wilson across the parking lot. "Wilson," I yelled, flagging him down as he got into his car to drive two more hours back to Tucson. "Please! Just come back inside and tell me what you're talking about." After some persuading, he did so, and once we got back inside, my first question was, "Okay, Wilson, how is this going to work?" He explained that his brother Bob, the president of Sundt, would be retiring in July. I was to report to the Tucson headquarters in August as the new president of Sundt Construction. I had unceremoniously been promoted from senior vice president and manager of Sundt's building division right to the chief operating officer's suite, which, until then, had only once been occupied by someone other than a member of the Sundt family. How on earth had this happened? While trying to fathom that my career dream was coming true, I realized I was in desperate need of a few more details. Wilson took a sheet of paper and drew his version of an organizational chart. He started with a big box near the top. "Here I am—CEO," he said, scrawling a bunch of smaller boxes orbiting around his. "I have all these ... groups ... that report to me." He drew lines from his box to every other group on the page. "So there you have it," he said, looking satisfied with his explanation of the inner workings of one of America's largest construction companies. Something was missing in Wilson's company picture. "Where am I on this?" I asked him. Wilson blinked in surprise at my obvious question. Then he scratched a box in the middle of where all the lines crisscrossed each other. "You'll be up here ... somewhere."

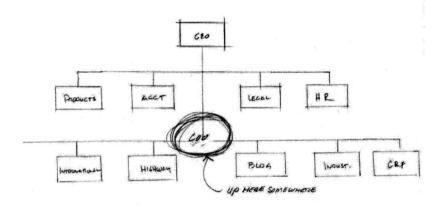

I had visions of being president of the company since I first started at Sundt. But now that the offer was right in front of me, that day, at that moment, I wasn't sure anymore.

When I started with Sundt in 1966, I was twenty-one years old and had an associate's degree in civil technology. Like all young people, I had aspirations to do something great with my life, but I just didn't know what. I was working for another company on a project in Arizona that Sundt was also on when I received an offer to become a field engineer for them. I started doing some research on Sundt to find out what they were all about. I got reports from the community, subcontractors, past and present employees, customers and anyone else who ever had contact with the company—and their responses were absolutely glowing.

For example, there was a local subcontractor who was getting the runaround from two other local contractors. He approached Bob Sundt and explained his situation. Bob asked him how much in the hole he was because of these contractors. The subcontractor told him he was owed sixty grand. Without another question asked, Bob called accounting and told them to cut the guy a check for $60,000—no invoice, just a check written on Bob Sundt's word.

"Bob paid my next month's billing based on my word!"

From that point on, whenever he bid Sundt, he always gave them an advantage just because of the enormous respect he had for the generosity and integrity Bob Sundt showed that day.

After enough over-the-top, rave reviews like this from anyone who had ever worked for or done business with the company, I wondered if Sundt Construction was for real. Was I on *Candid Camera*? This company sounded too good to be true.

Before I made my final decision on whether to take the job or not, I checked with one more person: the voice of wisdom in my life. I told my father about my job offer and what people were saying about Sundt. He told me in no uncertain terms that the character of the owners was a direct reflection of the caliber of the company. "Dad, I'm getting stories that they're as good as it gets," I said, still shaking my head in disbelief. "If they're that good, take the job, and you'll have a long and enjoyable career," he advised.

So, twenty-six years later, when Wilson offered me the Sundt presidency, I saw it as an honor and the achievement of my career goal. I accepted and began spending most of the week in the company's Tucson office, working out of a temporary cubicle I'd been assigned. It was only then that I realized I'd been given the helm of a sinking ship.

What I quickly discovered was that Sundt was losing millions of dollars.

I also learned that the company had a long list of construction claims and litigation. I started digging into finances at the operating level and realized what a dysfunctional, financially sick organization Sundt had become. I saw group after group, division after division that hadn't been consistently profitable for ten years. Why hadn't these groups been shut down? How did it get this bad? What had I become president of?

I have always enjoyed a challenge. Becoming president of a company was something I aspired to, but this was not exactly what I had dreamed of. Now I was just hoping I was up to the challenge that was ahead of us.

1993
Richard Condit
Senior Vice President and Chief Administrative Officer

The fact that Doug became president of this company *is* the reason we're telling the story of one of perhaps the most remarkable corporate turnarounds in history. As he mentioned earlier, when he was given the reins, Wilson Sundt, the CEO, wasn't really sure where Doug fit within the newly restructured organization now that his brother was retiring.

When Doug arrived at the Tucson headquarters in the summer of 1992, they didn't even have a place for him to sit, much less an executive office with his name on the door. For about six months he moved his things from conference room to conference room to empty cubicle until they finally found a suitable office for him. This experience in the end had a very positive impact on our company as it galvanized in Doug's mind that this was never going to happen again and led to his commitment to developing our people and providing for succession planning.

I should also note at this point that there were others within Sundt who had their eye on the presidency, so naturally they were disappointed when Doug got the job. His promotion also caused tension amongst the rank-and-file employees since any change in leadership can be a fearful experience as folks wonder how it will impact them personally.

Wilson's uncertainty that Doug was the right person for the job, the fact that Bob Sundt had run the building side of the business and had a better understanding of Doug's capabilities, and probably several other reasons unknown to us make it easier to understand why Wilson dragged his feet on the decision for as long as possible, balking against repeated recommendations by Bob and in particular our human resources director, Al Schifano, that Doug was absolutely the best candidate for the job. It can't be overstated how influential Al's belief in Doug was in having him named president. Sundt has benefited greatly from Al's belief in Doug and his tenacity in getting Wilson to share that belief at least to the degree that he made that trip to Phoenix that day in 1992. It sure helps to have an advocate!

In fact, the reason for Wilson's last-minute, two-hour drive up to Phoenix to promote Doug was that he had waited until the last minute to pull the trigger. I honestly think he used the drive to give himself one last chance to change his mind and turn the car around. But he didn't. When it came down to it, Wilson acquiesced because he trusted Bob and Al when they told him that Doug was the *only* one who could provide the leadership that was needed to address the issues the company was facing. In his heart of hearts, Wilson wanted what was best for his family's company. This trait of wanting what was best for the company was one of Wilson's many good qualities, and thank goodness that was the case, or I am convinced this story would not have had a happy ending.

I arrived at Sundt in 1993. Similar to Doug's reasons for coming to work here, my decision was greatly influenced by Sundt's stellar reputation in the community. When I mentioned to a friend that I was thinking of coming to work here, he said, "I was a tile layer for Sundt (a subcontractor). Richard, all you need to know is they pay their bills and play fair." I picked up very quickly that everyone had always respected Sundt's integrity throughout the history of the company. Just like Doug, I joined Sundt when it became clear that if I was going to make this significant change in my career, this was the company for me.

Doug had just taken the helm the previous year, and I quickly decided that he had the skill set and vision to make Sundt successful again. I eagerly took on the role of helping Doug become successful in his job because, honestly, he was the only one in my eyes who would be able to do what needed to be done, and I learned early on that Sundt was a company worth sustaining. Almost all of Doug's initial ideas as president ultimately led to the components of Sundt's turnaround. He understood he did not have all the skills he needed to turn the company around, and he committed himself to being a key observer of success in other organizations and trying those ideas at Sundt.

The thing that really struck me about Doug, however, was his passion for winning. The man does not like to lose. By the time he was named president, the proverbial "bar" at Sundt had been lowered so much that the company was mired in a culture where losing was accepted and quickly forgiven. Most people didn't pay much attention to the losses until we were nearly broke. Doug came along and changed that. He made it clear from the beginning that losing was not an option—no excuses. I saw immediately that with Doug running the ship, the bar was about to be set a whole lot higher. He was committed to making Sundt a winner again.

SECTION I

GREAT COMPANY— SERIOUS PROBLEMS

Chapter 1

HISTORY

We felt it was important to include a brief history of Sundt early in the book. A review of our history explains who we are and gives a glimpse into some of the important characteristics that were at play during the turnaround. For instance, our history is the reason that we enjoyed a great reputation at a time when the company was in serious trouble, and that certainly made the turnaround easier than if that had not been the case. The value and impact of corporate culture (strong or weak) on the current and future state of an enterprise will be something to pay attention to as you read this story and look to apply its lessons in your own company.

History, 1890–1990

The Start: M. M. Sundt
The First Generation: 1890–1929

Sundt's roots as a good company, built on solid underpinnings, start in 1890 with a young ship's carpenter from Norway. Mauritz Martinsen Sundt was born in Gjovik, Norway in 1863. At the age of twelve the young man who would become M. M. Sundt, the founder of Sundt Construction, joined Norway's merchant marine and sailed the Atlantic and Baltic seas for four years on windjammers. During that time he worked hard, perfecting his skills as a ship's carpenter, and diligently learning the tools of the trade. But when Mauritz's voyages eventually brought him to America, the lure of new challenges and promise of opportunity made him step onto dry land for good.

He settled for a short time in Wisconsin, married, and moved to Colorado for his health. Sadly, after their third child was born, his wife passed away from "mountain fever." M. M. sent his children to live with his wife's family in Wisconsin and relocated to Las Vegas, New Mexico Territory. Once settled, he sent for his children and began working as a carpenter for J. J. Hill, a local building contractor. Accompanying his children on the cross-country trip from Wisconsin was a woman who had been working for his wife's family. She stayed on in Las Vegas as M. M.'s housekeeper. They married a few months later and together had nine more children.

Within a few years, M. M. Sundt and coworker V. A. Henry bought out their employer and formed Henry & Sundt, Contractors and Builders. A few years later, M. M. bought out his partner and began doing business as M. M. Sundt, Builder. In 1910, the company was awarded its first major project: construction of a large dam in nearby Peterson Canyon for the Agua Pura Water Company. The fifty-five-foot-tall concrete dam was a landmark construction project for its time. It's important to note that it was built using muscle power—both animal and human—rather than the sophisticated construction machinery we are familiar with today. The entire project was completed for $21,843.

M. M. Sundt, Builder, soon became one of the prominent general contractors in the area, building homes, schools, government buildings, and business facilities. Much of the company's success was a direct reflection of Mauritz's high personal standards, honesty, and integrity. After all, in those days major project deals were often sealed with nothing more than a handshake and a man's word. Mauritz was a living example of a businessman who proved that "his word was his bond."

"Papa" Mauritz, set the bar high with an incredible work ethic, living by a strong set of core values and groundbreaking projects that put M. M. Sundt, Builder, on the Las Vegas map. We have both seen evidence of M. M. Sundt's legacy from our earliest days on the job here. All of us at Sundt today heard how M. M. Sundt was a man of high principles that guided his thinking and his actions. These principles became the seeds of our character as an organization, and they still exist in every corner of the company today. "Papa" Sundt's integrity meant a lot. It was the foundation and springboard for the entire company. Now it would be up for the next generation of Sundts to continue building upon that excellence.

The Second Generation: 1929–1965
Expansion to Arizona

In 1929 Mauritz learned that Sundt & Wenner, a design firm in Philadelphia, headed by his son Thoralf, had designed a new Methodist church to be built in Tucson, Arizona. Mauritz, a devout Methodist, wanted to be the one to build the church. He sent another of his sons, John, to Tucson with the company's bid. John had learned the carpentry trade from his father and had already been working for him in Las Vegas for several years. M. M. Sundt was the low bidder for the Methodist church. John stayed in Tucson to build it, picking up several other projects while he was there. When the church was finished, he decided to remain in Tucson, and for the next several years the Tucson and Las Vegas offices operated autonomously. When things were slow in Las Vegas, Mauritz would travel to Arizona to help his son. As time went on, this happened more and more frequently, as the Tucson operation was growing rapidly in size and reputation.

In 1936, with the country in the midst of the Great Depression, the University of Arizona began a major expansion of its campus in Tucson. This construction work would provide much-needed facilities for the school while also stimulating the depressed local economy. The project was funded by the Public Works Administration, a depression-era federal agency. M. M. Sundt was awarded a contract for six of the campus projects, all constructed simultaneously. Sometime during the 1930s, John bought out his father's interest and Tucson became the new headquarters for M. M. Sundt Construction Co. The original operation in Las Vegas became the company's New Mexico division.

Mauritz Sundt continued to work well into his seventies, occasionally taking up his carpenter tools to help out on a project here and there. The Sundt founder, who through his hard work and strong character had built an enterprise that would grow to be one of the nation's largest and most respected construction companies, died in Las Vegas on July 8, 1942, at the age of seventy-eight.

The War Years

By the time World War II broke out, M. M. Sundt Construction was well established as one of the leading general contractors in the Southwest. The federal government quickly pressed the firm into service for the war effort.

The company's biggest World War II-era challenge began at a secret meeting with U.S. government officials on December 1, 1942. Gene Sundt (a son of Joe Sundt, Mauritz's oldest child), was in charge of the New Mexico division by that time. Gene's recounting of that meeting reads more like a science fiction story than a business meeting. He was taken to a remote location in the mountains northwest of Santa Fe and told that his company had been selected to build a supersecret project at that location. All Gene could see in those mountains were the five log and stone buildings that made up a ranch school for boys.

The plans had not been completed, he was told, but Gene was provided with a list of buildings and told to get started right away. After the meeting, still having no idea what these buildings were for, Gene called his uncle, John

Sundt, and told him that the company had just been hired for a supersecret government building project that would run around $300,000, quite a large sum of money in those days. Thoralf Sundt joined the team to supervise design and engineering.

Over the following fourteen months, the original contract was modified seventy times for additional work the government wanted, including dams in two nearby canyons for a water supply; the pipelines to bring it to the site; streets; sewers; sewage treatment; power resources; housing for military and technical personnel; schools; hospitals; and the exacting and complicated buildings in the project's technical and testing facilities, both under and above ground. The building project had turned into construction of an entire city!

All of the work was completed on an almost impossible timetable despite the many hardships caused by secrecy, isolation, and the rugged terrain. By November 1943, Sundt's final contract with the U.S. government for this supersecret project had risen to a whopping $7.1 million. What were they building in the rugged mountains outside Santa Fe, New Mexico?

On August 6, 1945, those who worked on the project learned of its purpose, along with the rest of America. The first atomic bomb was dropped on Hiroshima, Japan, and the world could finally be told about the secret installation in New Mexico, known as Los Alamos. In the small city that Sundt had built for them, scientists with the Manhattan Project created the weapon that ended the war.

The years immediately after World War II were lean ones for the construction industry. The U.S.A. was shifting gears to a peace-time economy, and there wasn't much to build while that was taking place, but many important things were happening within M. M. Sundt Construction Co.

In 1948 Robert ("Bob") S. Sundt, one of Thoralf's sons, went to work for the company as a timekeeper and laborer during his summer break from the University of Arizona. Upon graduation two years later, he joined the company full-time, eventually rising all the way to the presidency. His father, Thoralf, remained with Sundt, serving as manager of the Building Department for almost twenty years before retiring in 1961.

The 1950s for M. M. Sundt were a time of expansion and diversification, as the company entered the heavy construction field. Over the ensuing years, M. M. Sundt would become one of the state's leading heavy construction contractors.

During the 1950s, M. M. Sundt grew rapidly, building schools, hospitals, retail stores, and a wide variety of projects for the industry. Sundt's military expertise was called into play repeatedly during this period for several critical projects, including construction of the first underground ballistic missile launching facility at Vandenberg Air Force Base in California (which later became the prototype for the Titan I Missile installations).

Another milestone in the family company occurred in 1957 when Bob's brother, H. Wilson Sundt, joined the firm. Also a University of Arizona graduate, Wilson undertook postgraduate studies in civil engineering to further prepare him for his career at Sundt. As was hinted at in the prologue, Wilson, like his brother Bob, also rose to the top ranks of the company. While Bob and Wilson and the rest of the younger generation at Sundt came into their own, the defining force of the second generation was John Sundt. Once he assumed leadership of the great company started by his father, he oversaw its rise to even greater heights.

Driven by John's leadership and strong entrepreneurial spirit, Sundt added highway work, industrial work, and sand, gravel, and concrete to its areas of expertise. As grand as John's entrepreneurial ventures were, he never once lost touch with the core values and beliefs that his father had instilled in him. His beliefs about things such as giving back to the community, investing in his employees, and living a life of integrity were a direct reflection of his father's. Tragically, the next era of Sundt was ushered in by John's sudden death from a heart attack in 1965 while game hunting in Africa. It would be up to the newest generation of Sundts to pick up the pieces of this great company and move forward.

The Third Generation: 1965–1998
Milestones, International Prominence, and Rapid Growth

Upon John Sundt's untimely death, the company moved quickly to establish new leadership. Fortunately, the management transition went smoothly, thanks to the wisdom and generosity of John Sundt's widow. When he died, she became the majority owner, but rather than sell the assets and close the company, or sell out to a competing firm, she chose to gift her stock to a group of managers and her family.

Since Bob and Wilson Sundt did not yet have enough management experience to run the company, longtime Sundt employees William Naumann and Duane Anderson were given the top leadership roles. Wilson Sundt became executive vice president and Bob Sundt became senior vice president and manager of the building division. A few years later, when both Naumann and Anderson were ready to retire, Wilson became chief executive officer and Bob took over as president. Bob and Wilson made it a priority, as the Sundts before them had, to keep the company's core values ever present and to continue to give back to the community (a top priority at Sundt, tracing back to M. M.).

Sundt in the Sixties

During the 1960s M. M. Sundt began to be recognized on both the national and international levels for its skill in completing large and complex projects with speed and efficiency. This era was marked by a dramatic expansion of the company's construction of ballistic missile facilities in particular, including the Atlas "F" complex of twelve missile silos at Schilling Air Force Base in Salina, Kansas, and the launch facilities for the Titan II ICBM at Vandenberg Air Force Base in California.

M. M. Sundt even had a hand in putting man on the moon. With a joint venture partner, the company built Launch Pad 39-A at Cape Canaveral Florida in 1965. The well-known facility would send Apollo 11 to the moon, was the launch pad for the fabled Apollo 13 flight, and launched the space shuttle Columbia decades later.

During this period of rapid growth, M. M. Sundt was also busy at home in Arizona. From building many of the highways that crisscross Arizona today to reaching new heights in the construction of high-rise office buildings and playing a key role in the growth of the state's mines and utilities, Sundt was making an impressive mark on the construction landscape. This was also the decade when Sundt ventured into the international marketplace. In 1962 the firm constructed sewage treatment facilities in Trinidad, West Indies. In 1966 Sundt expanded its reach, opening a regional office up the highway in Phoenix. Among that office's early projects were the Bureau of Indian Affairs Hospital and the Phoenix headquarters of the Empire Machinery Company.

1970s: Sundt Continues to Expand

The term *exponential growth* for what occurred at Sundt during the 1970s is an understatement. The company completed numerous successful projects, earned national recognition for its expertise in slipforming concrete building cores, and built additional landmark projects. Sundt also opened offices in the Philippines and Saudi Arabia, and made its first expansion into California with the acquisition of C. R. Fedrick, Inc.

Sundt also answered the need from Arizona's growing population for a dramatic expansion of the state's freeway system. At one point during the decade, M. M. Sundt was ranked as one of the ten largest builders of federal highway projects in the country. This was a good company that was growing fast! Near the end of the decade, more restructuring occurred, and Sundt Corp. was formed as a holding company for the expanding family of enterprises. One of the landmark events of the decade for Sundt was its work overseas in Saudi Arabia. In 1975 Arabian Sundt, Ltd. (Sundt in joint venture with two other enterprises) was awarded a management contract to build 485 condominiums in Saudi Arabia's eastern province for the Arabian American Oil Company. The following year the company received a $100 million labor and management contract for additional work, including the first highway bridge ever built in that part of Saudi Arabia. Ten years and many contract extensions later, the estimated total value of work put in place by Arabian Sundt was $750 million.

In 1972 Sundt took a crucial step toward becoming an employee-owned corporation by replacing the existing profit-sharing plan and trust with a stock bonus trust.

1980s

During this decade, the family of companies that was already recognized as one of the hundred largest construction organizations in the country continued to expand. The Sundt family of companies also continued building on its already impressive portfolio of projects for the industrial, electric utility, and heavy construction industries, as well as strengthening its presence in the international marketplace with projects in Chile, Australia, and the Philippines. Sundt continued to expand in California with the purchase of Ninteman Construction, a well-respected San Diego-based construction company founded in the 1940s The company also began working in northern California with joint venture partners. Later it would acquire Earl Construction and established a strong presence in that market as well.

Building a Great Reputation

As one of the hundred largest construction companies in America celebrated its hundredth birthday in 1990, a remarkable accomplishment for any company, the spirit and core values of Mauritz Sundt continued to permeate the organization. We are here today because of the integrity and core values of Sundt that have never once been compromised in bad times or good. It's normal for people to be critical of whomever happens to be at the top, but the one thing that we are never critical of, and always have respect for, is the kind of organization that the Sundt family created, one that is not driven by profits first and everything else next.

In 1990 Sundt was also recognized by Arthur Anderson Co. as Arizona's most admired privately held corporation, an honor we have received twice since then. Sundt was a good company, and it showed. These values parallel our personal values and that is probably true of most other Sundt employees. This is why we are here. For those of us who worked for the Sundt family business, those values became a part of our DNA. The name on the door is not Doug Pruitt or Richard Condit; it's Sundt. But with the tremendous respect we both have for the company, we have worked hard to ensure that the Sundt name will not be maligned in any way because of our decisions and actions. We want Sundt to continue to be known as a top professional organization, working to make our community and industry better. That's what Mauritz Sundt wanted, and it's up to us and the future generations of Sundt employees to respect and honor that legacy

Why have *we* decided to tell the story of the Sundt turnaround? There are many business books on the shelves by the Jack Welches and other Fortune 500 authors of the world. However, these may not be as relatable to the average reader. We are just a small to mid-sized firm out in Arizona that got in trouble and managed to find its way out again. But the elements of our story and the lessons we learned *are* relatable to all companies whether they are GEs, high-growth emerging enterprises, or family-owned small businesses. This story will hit home with a lot of business people who that think the turmoil we went through only happens to the big guys.

It's also true that many other companies have traveled to the edge of the abyss and back and have their own tales to tell about their journey. We encourage them to tell those stories as well because, for us, telling the story of our near downfall has been educational and enlightening.

Some of us have been through hell and back with this company. Therefore, our first purpose for telling our story is to cement this book in the institutional memory of our people today and in the future so hopefully they don't ever have to experience this again. The story of how we got into trouble, how we got out, how future generations can just as easily get into trouble, and hopefully how they can stay out of it, is a part of the Sundt company legacy.

Building Blocks

1) One of the most important contributors to the turnaround was clearly the company's great reputation within the industry and the communities where it worked. Without that, many of the necessary steps to improvement would not have been possible.

   a) What is your company's current reputation or perception in the marketplace?

   b) Are there characteristics that you can capitalize on in your efforts to improve?

   c) Are there issues that are negatively impacting your reputation that may need more immediate attention?

2) A company's values and traditions are generally established by the founder and the first few generations of leaders. Each company has its own values, and one set is not necessarily any better or worse than another. But they do provide the foundation for strategies and decisions.

   a) What are your company's values and traditions?

   b) Are your values shared among all employees, or merely artifacts posted on the wall?

   c) Are employees and managers held accountable for demonstrating the company's values in the regular course of the company's business?

3) Sundt clearly had the potential for an early demise when John Sundt passed away unexpectedly. Many family-owned businesses fail because of poor succession planning or because later generations are not interested in the family business. Fortunately, John Sundt's widow allowed the company to continue and an orderly transition of leadership took place.

a) If you are a new or small company have you created a succession plan?

b) Are you working to develop potential future leaders for your company?

c) Do you have individuals in key positions whose unexpected departure would create significant issues?

Chapter 2

THE EDGE
OF THE ABYSS

How did a good company get into so much trouble?

Ironically, the impressive, storied Sundt history that you just read played a huge role in bringing us blindly to the edge of an abyss. As can often be the case in life and business, our greatest assets can sometimes become our greatest liabilities. There was no starter pistol to officially signal the beginning of our downward slide. Instead, it was a series of small, hardly discernable steps, fueled by our belief that we were too good a company to get in trouble. The expression bandied about these days, "too big/good to fail," accurately described our way of thinking for many years.

The core values that M. M. instilled, and the entire company took pride in, became a double-edged sword. They led to a belief that we were such a good company with such strong values and a long list of great feats that we were business royalty. In a word, we had become arrogant. And when you start to think you're better than everyone else and don't need to get better, that's the time when you are perilously close to failing. It's important to celebrate your past accomplishments, but your past will never define your future. We started resting on our laurels, hanging our hats on those accomplishments, and assuming that the future would work itself out. By 1992 we were on the brink of paying the ultimate price for our arrogant assumptions. We were going broke.

In Doug's words:

When I became president of Sundt in 1992, we had just closed the books on our worst loss in history. You immediately start asking the hard questions that clearly weren't being asked before: Why did we have such a big loss? What happened? How do you get to become president of a large company and not know how bad it truly was? We were on the edge of an abyss, teetering, and I was the one tasked with keeping us from falling in.

The financials were tightly held at Sundt. People usually knew what their own division was doing in great detail, but because each operated autonomously, what they knew about the other groups in the company was quite vague. We only knew that some were doing well, others were doing okay, and still others were not doing well at all. In the case of the latter group, we didn't know exactly how poorly they were actually performing. It wasn't the job of individual division leaders to look over the fence at the details of why the others were not making money. We kept our eyes on our own business, focused on managing our own work properly and doing a good job. This "siloed" thinking had both a good and a bad side. As mentioned, we were focused on running our businesses, which was the good side, but the bad side of that was we had no idea that the wheels were falling off in another area, and as a result leadership was not held accountable and we could not focus the collective will of the company on our problems.

Meanwhile, on the other side of the fence, the grass was not greener. Sundt Products, for instance, had essentially not made any money in ten years. The industrial division had not made much money in a long time. The highway division was also performing poorly and losing money. Ownership of the equipment fleet was costing us a significant amount of money. These were all problems that needed to be addressed, yet a blind eye was being turned toward them. We had people going in every direction, doing their own thing their own way with little if any controls. It was as if we were essentially several different companies held together by a common logo.

When I took the reins, it became crystal clear that we were a very dysfunctional organization. If you stuck all the problems Sundt was facing up on a board and looked at them together, you would quickly see that we had a good company that was in big trouble.

How far back did it go? When did the downward spiral begin? Obviously this is not something that can easily be pinpointed in business. Many of the biggest problems we were facing started out small and festered unnoticed under the surface. There was no solid system in place to spot and eliminate them. From the late 1960s into the 1970s and 1980s, Sundt was moving forward quickly, growing, developing, and performing very well on a multitude of projects. Those projects were being managed by extremely talented division leaders. But eventually these leaders retired, and many of their key leadership teams retired with them. Some had trained the people underneath them to step into their shoes seamlessly by giving them the skill sets they needed to succeed. But most, unfortunately, failed to undertake any sort of succession planning or training. Often when those successful division leaders retired, the people below them simply did not have the discipline and skill sets to carry the torch forward. Rather than looking for the best or most well-trained person as a replacement, division heads were being replaced by people "who had been here thirty years, and therefore it was their opportunity." There was little preparation for succession, and things quickly started to unravel.

Then there were the excuses and denial being thrown at the problems: You don't understand; this is how it is; you just don't get it because you're a building guy, not a highway guy; you're not one of us. We heard it all. But the fact remained that as a company we were losing millions of dollars and inexplicably failing to act to solve the problem.

A few years before 1992 the deterioration of Sundt was coming to a head.

Here we were, this mid-sized construction company in Arizona that had pulled off huge, successful, notable projects, failing because the arrogance of our success was keeping us from looking in the mirror. There was a real reluctance to deal with the ugly facts, including the fact that no matter how great you are, you still need to be open to change. It was like the evil witch in Snow White, looking in the mirror that she had preprogrammed to tell her only the good things about herself.

In 1992 I had walked into a hornet's nest of claims and litigation. The company was losing a significant amount of money, yet refusing to change. We were financing our losses through the strength of our balance sheet, which wasn't that strong and adding more debt. Both were destroying what financial integrity we had left as a company. I was frustrated because I believed I knew what needed to be done to right the ship, but I found few willing to support me in the hard decisions that needed to be made.

As you learned in the prologue, the two members of the Sundt family who were at the helm were Bob Sundt and his brother Wilson. Bob and Wilson were very different men as individuals, but as brothers they both had tremendous pride in their family and in the company.

Bob, the elder of the two, was more of a detail-oriented, t-crossing and i-dotting leader. As president of the company, he spent a lot of time personally making sure that the correct processes were set up to do the job right, every time. He was especially involved during the 1970s when Sundt was completing its first groundbreaking projects in Saudi Arabia. Bob was the one who would roll up his sleeves, taking a hands-on role in ensuring that the proper time was spent and details were attended to.

He also played a large role in Sundt's innovation. For instance, when we entered the fiberglass form market, Bob's efforts helped put us out in front of the industry, in both form design and the use of these forms for various types of concrete construction. The innovation didn't stop there. Bob also ramped up our scheduling tools, placing us way ahead on the technological curve before the days of fancy scheduling software. We were using computerized scheduling when computers were far from mainstream in our industry.

Wilson, on the other hand, loved to take risks as much as his brother loved taking care of the details. Some of his risks paid off in the form of pioneering projects that put Sundt on the industry map. Others, however, were a bit more costly but were still an admirable reflection of his big thinking. It was as if Wilson were seeing things from the 30,000-foot level, while Bob worked in the trenches. They tempered each other in this way, Wilson pushing Bob to take some risk, and Bob pushing on the brakes to do things right. We were starting to experience some significant problems in the late '80s that weren't being properly addressed because of the difference between Bob and Wilson. When Bob retired, the checks and balances that resulted from their different leadership styles went away and the wheels started to come off rapidly. Dealing with our failures became very difficult because we didn't want to face the music and make the painful decisions that needed to be made. What had kept Wilson and Bob together was their love and pride in this company and doing the right thing for their employees.

Another common characteristic of both Sundt brothers and a direct reflection of M. M. was their compassion. If there was an issue with an employee, both of their hearts really showed through. Wilson in particular was the first to be there for any employee who was suffering through a hardship.

Wilson's good nature sometimes overruled his business sensibilities. During the mid '90s, for example, we had to shut down Sundt Products because it was losing money [see Chapter 9 for more details on how fixing, selling and closing nonperforming assets was a key piece of Sundt's turnaround]. Well, much to my surprise, shortly afterwards, when I visited Sundt International, another one of our subsidiary companies, all the Sundt Products people were there! Wilson did not have the heart to let them go, so he simply relocated them. That was the heart of Wilson. From a business standpoint it was very frustrating. But as a human being it was hard not to respect the guy for his values; his heart was obviously in the right place.

Admittedly, making the hard decisions like laying people off is not supposed to be easy. But when business is struggling, as a leader you have to bite the bullet and do what needs to be done so the company can survive.

In the meantime, however, Sundt was quickly failing, and immediate and drastic actions needed to be taken to save the company. The Titanic was sinking, and everyone was dancing to the band. The hundred-plus-year-old company was stuck in a state of denial.

After Wilson left my office that day in 1992, following his announcement that I would be the new president, I was thrilled. I was going to be president of one of the greatest, most well-respected construction companies in the country and in the community! I went home, told my wife and we celebrated …

Sadly, I soon learned that I'd been sheltered in Phoenix because for the most part I had been running my own company and depositing the money into the Tucson headquarters. I had enjoyed a great career, and it was a rude awakening when I learned that we were facing the largest losses in Sundt history.

How could such a good company almost fail? The common denominators of our troubled years were: Multiple losses, litigation, lack of focus, loss of discipline, arrogance, lack of training, failure to create succession plans, and lack of leadership. Let's look at some of those areas.

First, there was a lack of discipline. We did have policies at Sundt, but even the few we had were in many cases being ignored. Construction is not rocket science, but it is risky and requires constant attention to discipline. Richard likes to use the illustration of an airline pilot to demonstrate the consequences of losing discipline. How would you like to get on a plane with a pilot who has already taken off five times that day and therefore decides that there is no need to do the preflight checklist this time? He forgets one little step, such as the proper setting of the flaps, and you and the plane are essentially done for on takeoff. An extreme example, but in a low margin business like ours, the financial consequences can be great if you lose discipline and fail to follow procedures. It's like climbing a twenty-story building. When you start skipping steps, hitting every third one, you're eventually going to stumble, and it's going to hurt. At Sundt, we were skipping steps, leaving steps out, and overall acting incredibly undisciplined as a company. We eventually paid the price, and it hurt.

From a process standpoint, it was obvious that there were no clear organizational systems in place either. Everyone was doing their own thing, their own way. Because there was no standardization between the various Sundt divisions, most of our business processes were being done seven different ways, causing huge inefficiencies. I think during this time we learned that our payroll department was receiving and processing fifteen different time-sheet forms. On top of that, this disjointed way of doing business was being promoted and encouraged within the organization because we truly believed each group was different! The unintended consequences of that leadership style were that disorganization had become the chosen way at Sundt.

Like many organizations, over the years we had built up many paradigms about how things were done at Sundt, and no one ever seemed to challenge the status quo. As a result, we drifted further from one of the defining values of our culture: innovation. We just got too comfortable with doing the things the way we had always done them, and few in the company saw challenging the status quo as career enhancing. For instance, we owned a lot of heavy equipment (loaders, scrapers, paving equipment, etc.) because, frankly, we just believed, like many other contractors, that this was the way to do business. This was a project-centered paradigm based on the belief that we could be more competitive if we owned our equipment rather than rent it. That sounds great in theory, but in reality we had a lot of equipment with very low utilization rates, and our equipment fleet was losing money every year. (We'll talk more about that in Chapter 9.) The way we used to view our equipment fleet is a great example of our having a strongly held paradigm that kept us from making the changes that would have allowed us to improve our performance. Jim Collins, in his book Good to Great, found that one of the characteristics of great companies was their willingness to address the "brutal facts." Clearly one of the reasons we were failing as a company was our inability to challenge the status quo and create a culture where there were mechanisms to ensure the brutal facts were apparent.

It was also glaringly clear, as we found ourselves on the edge of the abyss with no bridge across, that we had done a very poor job at succession planning. We had very talented people making money for their divisions, but when they retired, we learned that the group behind them was not adequately trained or developed to run the division successfully. There is a huge difference between running a project or putting an estimate together and running an entire division of the company profitably and effectively. We were doing a very poor job of making sure that individuals who were excellent at a specific function were being trained to understand and be competent in running an entire organization. Across the board, our failure to prepare our future leaders was causing divisions to falter, get in trouble, and lose more and more money.

From 1992 through 1995 we spent a lot of time trying to settle a host of claims while constantly asking, "Why are we in this claim in the first place?" The good news about the claim situation is that as we worked to resolve those claims, some of the root issues that had been eating at our performance became evident. Overall, a lack of discipline, focus, and training, which went on for years, led us into work that we should never have been in. What resulted, for the most part, were construction disputes with our subcontractors over scope of work and responsibilities, or contractual disputes with our customers.

Construction tends to be a fairly litigious industry. However, if you are proactive and address issues early when they're often small, those problems can typically be solved. If we had practiced this approach and stayed disciplined and focused, we might have eliminated 98 percent of the claims we had to deal with during those years. Some were with clients we never should have worked for in the first place because of their reputations. Other claims concerned projects we never should have pursued for a variety of reasons, including projects that the owner of the property had not properly financed. We wasted a lot of resources and dollars going through several unproductive years of costly litigation hell, all because we were chasing the wrong clients and the wrong jobs. It should be noted that in our industry the pressure to get work is extreme. When this is the case, you have to pay very close attention to ensure that those who get the work remain disciplined. In many cases it would have been less costly to have paid our people to stay home than to have taken the job.

These issues and others were quickly creating other problems. As you learned in Chapter 1, Sundt had always been known for its high quality of work. Unfortunately some of the things that were threatening the company's stability caused the quality of some project elements to slip, fortunately for us, not dramatically. From an estimating standpoint, jobs weren't as well thought out and planned as they had been before, and we took on projects and risk we shouldn't have. In our business, bad jobs and risks that have not been properly analyzed can lead to claims and litigation (as we saw).

We were growing as a company in terms of the projects we were taking on, but in the process we forgot to grow as an organization. There was a serious lack of investment in training, development, succession planning, and technology, and we needed to deal with this. Our new leaders were not prepared to lead. We were like the driver of a giant car who has one foot on the gas as he heads toward the ravine, and everyone was just going along for the ride. It was time for someone to start stepping on the brakes and getting things under control.

Building Blocks

1) Often, a company's greatest assets can become its greatest liabilities. Business failure is frequently not a single major event, but a series of small unnoticed steps that accumulate into serious issues. Companies begin to think they are too big or too good to fail. That was clearly true of Sundt as the company rested on its outstanding reputation but failed to actively manage the business for future success.

   a) Are there characteristics of your business that you are taking for granted that are sowing the seeds of future problems or issues?

   b) Are managers and employees complacent or blind to early warning signs of future problems?

   c) Are you reading and believing too many of your own press releases and not candidly assessing your situation?

2) As companies grow and expand, they frequently become a collection of separate organizations with a common logo. That was true of Sundt where the individual divisions operated quite autonomously.

These functional "silos" paid attention to their own business and their own financials, but generally did not know about (or care about) the financial success of other parts of the company.

a) Do the managers of the organizational units within your company view themselves as part of the whole, or are they only concerned with their own operations?

b) Are financials for the company as a whole shared with managers and employees so they can be part of the solution?

c) Are organizational units within your company willing and able to share people, information, and resources in a manner than benefits the company as a whole?

3) Lack of discipline was clearly one of the major contributors to Sundt's problems. In the name of "operational flexibility" the company allowed divisions and even those working on individual construction projects to create their own policies and procedures. In a low-margin business like construction, lack of discipline can create significant financial consequences.

a) Is discipline important in your business and your markets?

b) Do you pay attention to your operational policies and procedures to keep them current?

c) What aspects of your current business have lost the discipline necessary to be successful and sustainable, and what can you do to correct that?

Chapter 3

LINE IN THE SAND

In Richard's words:

There's nothing like being the captain of a ship you're not allowed to steer. True, Wilson Sundt had named Doug as company president and Bob Sundt's successor in 1992, but Wilson remained the CEO and, purposely or not, had effectively created a wall of resistance to the changes we needed to make to ensure Sundt's survival. The most vital change that needed to happen was to open the books, become more transparent and let employees know the dire straits we were in as a company. We needed an event … a come-to-Jesus moment where we revealed what we knew, and most importantly gave everyone the opportunity to join us in turning the company around and moving forward. You can't help solve what you don't know exists.

Doug intuitively knew he needed to get this message out and communicate to the company what was going on. We decided that this message would be conveyed at a transformative event of some kind. And thus the idea of Gold

Canyon was born. Doug went to Wilson with idea of a leadership meeting to let them know the true condition the company was in so they could get engaged in fixing the problems we faced. Wilson was not supportive of the concept.

> *Richard had the idea of asking for forgiveness rather than permission. There was an element of risk because if the meeting hadn't gone well, or Wilson hadn't liked what we did, I would have probably been fired. (Richard would probably have been spared. Maybe that's why he had the idea.) At that point I would have hated to lose my job, but I also didn't want to be there watching the ship sink and not being able to do something about it.*
>
> Doug

Gold Canyon is the name of the resort where we held a management retreat in the summer of 1996. In the months prior we delved into the planning, having numerous conversations about the goals of the meeting, the structure, who would be invited, and all the prep work that would be required to ensure we had all the data we needed to effectively present the problem and work toward a solution. Our CFO, Ray Bargull, who had become an important ally and played an important role in educating Doug on the specifics of our financial situation when he became president, was very valuable in getting us prepared for Gold Canyon.

When planning our agenda for the retreat, we anticipated that we would need to, at some point, open the books on the true financial circumstances of the company, but just as importantly, start engaging those in attendance in the question of what to do about it. We would need to set aside time for the company's leadership to talk about what was happening and start formulating a plan to solve these problems and right the ship again. The final agenda for Gold Canyon reflects these goals.

AGENDA

Tuesday, August 6

7:30 am	Continental Breakfast
8:00	Welcome and Introductions ....Participants
8:15	Building a Better Company -- One Job at a Time ....Doug Pruitt Ray Bargull
10:15	Break
10:30	Breakout Session (Assigned Groups) .... Richard Condit How can we, as managers, provide leadership toward:

- Pride
- Competence
- Responsibility

11:30	Breakout Session Reports ....Group Leaders
11:50	Personal Planning Activity .... Richard Condit
12:00	Lunch (on your own)
1:30 p.m.	Golf Scramble (for those registered)..Roger George Other Social Activities (your choice)
6:30	Reception ....Participants
7:00	Cook-Out "Kickin' Dirt – Tellin' Lies" ....Participants

Wednesday, August 7

7:30 am	Continental Breakfast	
8:00	Review of Yesterday	Doug Pruitt
8:15	Preview of Management Training Program	David Muehlbauer
8:45	ESOP Presentation	Ray Bargull
9:15	Break	
9:30	Breakout Sessions – Unit Strategic Planning	David Muehlbauer
12:00	Lunch (Sunrise Room)	
1:00 p.m.	Breakout Session Reports	Division/Department Managers
2:30	Committee Structure	Doug Pruitt
2:50	Recapitalization	Doug Pruitt
3:15	Break	
3:30	Panel Discussion	Rick Buchanan Roger George Brian Murphy Tom Remensperger Bill Zeiss
4:30	Closing and Conference Evaluation	Doug Pruitt
5:00	Adjournment	

Thursday, August 8

7:30 a.m.	Continental Breakfast
8:00	Team 2000 Strategic Planning
12:00	Lunch
1:00 p.m.	Team 2000 (Continued)
?	Adjournment

The meeting was going to be, in large part, a bully pulpit where Doug could lay out where we were and some of his thoughts on what we needed to do about it. We wanted to get people engaged in solutions right away, so we included breakout sessions in smaller groups to brainstorm how each person could help solve the problems we were facing and improve their leadership skills. The finale would be at the end of day two, when each person in attendance would be asked to individually decide how committed they were to sticking with us, weathering the storm and working with us to solve problems. The curtain was about to go up on Gold Canyon, and we had no idea what kind of reviews we were about to receive.

Come to Jesus

Gold Canyon is an older resort, outside the Phoenix urban center and far away from the comfort zone of the Sundt offices. We chose it for this reason, so the company leaders in attendance could not escape back to work at a moment's notice (cell phones were not prevalent back then). The resort was also extremely affordable (especially key in light of the financial situation we were about to reveal).

The resort is set at the base of Arizona's Superstition Mountains, loaded with their fair share of mysterious folklore. As the story goes, a German immigrant named Jacob Walzer, who would later come to be known as the Lost Dutchman, found a mine full of gold that he kept secret until his dying day in 1891. Then, on his deathbed, he finally revealed his secret to a boarding-house owner named Julia Thomas, who had been caring for him for years. The actual mine has never been found, but that never stopped locals and gold-seeking tourists alike from taking their shot at uncovering the Dutchman's gold.

On August 6, 1996, our admittedly unpolished group of about forty-nine leaders from across the various divisions of Sundt arrived at the base of the Superstition Mountains, the place where many people had come searching for treasure and many had not survived. We had no idea how our come-to-Jesus meeting would turn out, and how many of the original group would survive in the long run, or whether this might be the place we would find our pot of gold. It was time to open the books, become transparent, tell the truth, and find out. Included in that group, perhaps reluctantly but still present, was Wilson Sundt.

Once we convened on day one, it was interesting to note how much it looked like a group of total strangers meeting for the first time. These were forty-nine people who all led various divisions in the same medium-sized company and many of whom had never met one another. When we got together for that first session, people were greeting each other with, "Hi, I've heard your name but I'd never met you." People knew very little about what was happening outside their own group. They all worked in separate silos under one company logo.

Is it any wonder that these people were so in the dark about the condition of the company when they barely knew what was happening outside their own office? The company's long-standing closed-book policy was killing their livelihoods, and nobody even knew we were on life support.

Once the pleasantries and introductions were done, it was time to get down to business. It was time to open the books and face the consequences. We placed the financials of a highly leveraged, poorly performing construction company in front of everyone. The sea of faces in that resort meeting room registered absolute shock. They were hearing financial realities about Sundt for the very first time, and most couldn't believe things were so bad in the good company they worked for.

The questions started flying from across the room: Are you saying that we're bankrupt? Is our reputation keeping us afloat? How could this happen to the company, our company, a company that has been around for so long and done so well? These were the same questions that Doug had been asking himself when he became president and were now being presented to the people in the meeting room.

It was a very emotional moment when Doug told everyone in the room that as a company, we were dying. The day after Gold Canyon, someone in my department came into my office with tears in his eyes. He thought he had a career for life here, but now he wondered if there would be a Sundt much longer.

Once the moment of initial shock had passed, it was time to work together to save the sinking ship. We broke out into groups of departments. Even in the groups, people were still reeling, trying to reconcile this new, disturbing picture of their company with the one they thought they worked for. Nevertheless, there was work to be done. The human resources group discussed skill sets that needed to be ratcheted up. Accounting talked about the importance of improving billing and collection procedures. The operating divisions started discussing what they needed to do to make sure we could take on projects and complete them with a high degree of quality and good profitability.

Each group was tasked with creating new solutions for the problems they had just found out about earlier in the day. Despite the emotions, the group sessions, as well as subsequent ones, were surprisingly productive. We saw that when people are emotional about something they become motivated to take action. Gold Canyon had already become a catalyst for a turnaround.

The Line in the Sand

In Doug's words:

As the sun was starting to set on Gold Canyon on the last day of the retreat, we arrived at the moment of truth; ; it was come-to-Jesus time. Standing at the podium, under a project slide that discussed a line-in-the-sand analogy, I delivered my closing remarks to the assembled leadership of Sundt:

"You have heard over the last couple of days what the problems are. We need to go in a different direction. I don't have all the answers, but collectively, as a leadership group, it is our responsibility to protect shareholder value and fix this thing. This is not one person's responsibility; it's our collective responsibility. We are going to move forward with this company; that's a fact. We're going to make a lot of changes. You're not going to like a lot of them, because they are going to be counter to how you are used to running things. If you're not willing to change, you won't be here. You may not survive this onslaught of change. We may ask you to go home. We're going to change. We have no choice."

At that point I paused and surveyed the room. I noticed Wilson, sitting quietly in the very last row by himself. How would Wilson Sundt, the proud, stubborn CEO of the company and last remaining family member in power at Sundt, react to what was about to happen? "I need to know if you're going to be a part of the solution. If you don't want to participate in this challenge, that's okay, but this is not the place for you to be." Then, I pointed at the line on the floor where the carpeting met the wooden floor of the stage. "Here is a mythical line in the sand. Who will join me on this side of that line and go about the business of fixing this great company?"

In Richard's words:

Dave Muehlbauer, our corporate director of training, and I knew what was coming. Dave and I agreed that as much as we wanted to, we would not jump up and be the first ones to cross the line and join Doug on the stage. We felt it was more important for others to go up there first. But what happened next shocked us all.

The words were barely out of Doug's mouth, when from the very back row, Wilson sprung to his feet and hustled toward the stage. Our jaws dropped! Several days before Gold Canyon, when Doug and I were talking about how Wilson might react to what was going to be presented, we weren't sure he would even show up, let alone cross a metaphorical line in the sand. And here he was, breaking speed records to make absolutely certain that he was the first one to cross that line and stand by Doug's side. This was an astonishing show of total loyalty and solidarity from Wilson, and no one saw it coming. In hindsight, however, it makes a lot of sense. Wilson was a very bright guy, and he knew this was simply the right thing to do to save his beloved company from certain demise.

Then, to our continued amazement, Wilson said to those gathered in the room, "This is a great company. Don't let it fail." Guess what everyone else did immediately. Chairs were quickly pushed back, and with no words spoken, every person in that room joined Doug, shoulder to shoulder, on the stage. As Wilson stood there next to Doug the leadership baton had been very visually passed to Doug. It would be several more years before Wilson would retire but Doug took the reins of the company that evening in 1996.

As the meeting concluded, the famous Gold Canyon group photo was snapped. We say famous because within a few years about 60 percent of those people were no longer with the company. Some left, a couple retired, others were fired, and unfortunately one died.

1996 leadership academy

Sometimes the hardest, yet most important thing to do is leave behind the people who may have contributed under one set of circumstances but were not going to be helpful in the future. But for that moment, the picture represented the commitment of each person there to face the extraordinary challenge of turning around an extraordinary company and bring it back from the abyss to greatness again.

In Doug's words:

What I realized is that most people in leadership knew we had problems, but had no clue as to their depth and breadth. I honestly didn't believe we had any chance of making the changes we needed to make unless we could have that discussion and get the real numbers in front of everyone. (As James Collins would say, "deal with the brutal facts.") In hindsight, Gold Canyon turned out to be a major event in Sundt's history. My biggest fear was that when I gave my line-in-the-sand challenge, no one would get up. If they hadn't accepted that challenge, Gold Canyon would have still gone down as a famous event in Sundt's history, but in a very different way. Thank God they got up and crossed that line in the sand and accepted the challenge.

Transition of Leadership

Gold Canyon could not possibly have had a better outcome, and this was largely due to Wilson's finale. Would everyone else have crossed that line without his grand gesture of loyalty to the company? Who knows? Maybe Wilson understood this because he knew that most of the people in that room were still more loyal to him than to Doug, and they would not have crossed the line without him.

But truly, we did not realize how important Gold Canyon was to Sundt's future at the time it was unfolding. It opened the books. It let people know what and where the problems were so we could focus on solving them together. It sent the message loud and clear that we were no longer going to be a bunch of silos anymore; we were going to come together as one collaborative company, and years later, that's exactly what we are.

It also provided a visual transition of leadership from Wilson to Doug. Of course this wasn't an instantaneous, clean transition that occurred the moment after Gold Canyon ended. People were still going to Wilson first for key decisions. However, it did provide a springboard to get people engaged and dealing with problems. Gold Canyon set the bar higher, and past behaviors and performance would no longer be acceptable in the future.

Sometimes you do things: you make decisions, you take action, and you do what it takes to survive and move forward. At the time you do these things you don't know which ones will work and which won't. Gold Canyon was the right thing, done in the right way, at the right time. This was one of the most significant events in our company's history and was instrumental in everything that has happened since. Those remarkable two days at the foot of the legendary Superstition Mountains were the true starting point of our turnaround, and to some degree we were on our way to finding our own pot of gold.

After Gold Canyon we continued to hold annual leadership academies. Now over a hundred people come together each time for a two-and-a-half-day retreat, focused on continuing our efforts to improve the company. The academies are designed to ensure we can meet our goals in the future so Sundt can successfully see its next 120 years.

After Gold Canyon, Wilson essentially began to step aside and was having less and less to say about all of the changes that were being made. It appeared that his actions at Gold Canyon in being the first to cross the line were sincere. Wilson loved this company that his family had built, and in his heart of hearts knew it was time to let others give leadership to those changes. The real challenge was to determine what, in Wilson's mind, were the issues that needed to be satisfied for him to make his decision to retire.

Of course one of those issues was starting to be satisfied as it appeared Wilson was starting to be comfortable with the idea that Doug was the guy for the role. Doug, on the other hand, was very frustrated as from his perspective he was not the president of the entire company, only certain parts. One of the problems was that other managers were still going around Doug to Wilson, which to a large degree was understandable since Wilson had not told them otherwise.

In Doug's words:

I hadn't started looking for work elsewhere, but about a year after Gold Canyon I got a very good job offer that I was considering. My wife basically said she would support my decision to change jobs and move if necessary, but if I left and this company went under, I would hate myself for not staying and doing whatever I could to make it work out. Needless to say, I stayed. I owe her a great deal of gratitude for her wisdom.

Richard also knew I was considering another job, and he and Ray Bargull went to work trying to figure out how to accelerate the succession of leadership from Wilson to me. They were successful in that effort. The employees of Sundt owe them a great deal of gratitude for their courage.

In Richard's words:

In 1997 I identified Bob Petrello as someone who might be able to help me figure out how to make this transition successful. Bob was suggested by the director of the leadership program several of us had participated in at the Center for Creative Leadership in San Diego. We originally wanted that individual to help, but he said, "No, you don't want me, you want this guy named Bob Petrello," the man who had been in his position at the Center for several years before leaving to start his own firm. So reluctantly I flew to San Diego to meet Bob. As I was introduced to this long-haired, Birkenstock-wearing hippie who was Bob Petrello, I thought, "Wilson is never going to go for a guy who looks like this!" Despite these misgivings, Bob had come to us highly recommended, so we hired him. It was now time for the hippie to meet Wilson.

We finally got Wilson to meet with him by telling him that we had hired a coach to "help Doug get ready to meet his expectations," but Wilson would need to meet with him first. Once that meeting started, it was truly remarkable how quickly Bob peeled back the onion and showed us what Wilson was really thinking and what things needed to be done for him to feel comfortable and retire. It was obvious that he was overwhelmed and wanted to protect Doug by not putting too much on his plate at one time.

From that point on, the turnaround and handing over of the reins moved relatively quickly, with Ray Bargull and I addressing the issues that Bob Petrello had uncovered in his conversation with Wilson, paving the way for his retirement in 1999, when Doug became chairman and CEO.

The bottom line, and another basic of business, was that Wilson knew what needed to be done to execute a successful corporate turnaround, but he just did not have the wherewithal to do it. Doug had the courage to make the tough decisions needed to right the ship again.

Building Blocks

1) For Sundt, and in particular for Doug and Richard, the turning point was the leadership conference held at the Gold Canyon Resort. It was a time to let the managers in the company understand the serious issues facing the company and enlist their support. The call to cross the line in the sand was a defining moment to get people involved in the solution and (unexpectedly) for Doug to get a signal from Wilson Sundt that he could lead the company.

    a) Does your company need a come-to-Jesus event to candidly share the current state and get people involved in the changes needed?

    b) Do you (or other senior leaders) need to be more open with other managers about the current financial situation within the company?

    c) Do you need to get a solid and tangible commitment for senior managers to be part of the team and part of the solution?

2) Securing the assistance of an outside consultant, specifically Bob Petrello, was a key to the transformation. There are certainly thousands of consultants and consulting organizations in the marketplace and finding the right team or person is not easy. Sundt was very lucky to find just the right person for that time in our company's history and his impact has been significant.

    a) Do you need to find competent outside consulting help for your company?

    b) Have your clearly defined the key business or leadership issues you need to address before starting your search?

    c) Do you have business associates or colleagues who can help you in your search to find the right person/team for your businesses unique situation?

3) Even after Gold Canyon some managers continued to go around Doug and take problems and decisions to Wilson. And Doug still reported to Wilson. At this point, Richard and Doug decided that there were times when they would need to "ask for forgiveness rather than permission." This strategy always comes with certain risks, but it was frequently the right approach during this transition.

   a) Are you still waiting for permission?

   b) Are there things you need to do to help your organization become successful that you should just do and ask forgiveness if they fail?

   c) Are you aware of and willing to take the risk to do that?

SECTION II

THE TURNAROUND YEARS, 1996–2004

THE TURNAROUND YEARS

> *These are the years where I really partnered with Doug. Most of the other people were still wrapped up in their own silos, and there were not a lot of people willing to tackle the bigger problems the company was facing. It became clear to me that I could help Doug get done what he wanted to do. We were a rudderless ship and we needed to plan and manage our company more strategically. I saw in Doug a leader with a vision for Sundt, and I saw it as my job to help him be successful, if I could, and help to ensure this wonderful company would thrive for another 120 years."*
>
> Richard

In this section of the book we identify the key components of the turnaround. You are not going to find any silver bullets but rather the execution of some basic best practices in running a good business. It is remarkable how far Sundt had deviated from the common sense basics of running a business. It is so easy to develop blinders about what is really happening and how quickly you can begin the slide toward the abyss.

The great football coach Vince Lombardi said, "Winning is a habit, unfortunately so is losing." Back in the late 1980s and early 1990s, there was a habit of losing at Sundt. We both heard a lot of "this is a high risk, tough business. You win some, you lose some, and at the end of the day you eke out a little profit," and that's exactly what we were doing. You are what you think, and since losing was an accepted part of the game, we had a long string of jobs that lost money. Losing was ingrained into our culture, I recall a conversation with a manager on a project who told me when I asked him if he had a profitable job, he replied, "we're doing fine, I don't think we will lose any money." He wasn't even thinking about making a profit. The goal to him was not losing anything.

When you win as an organization, your customers, employees, projects, and subcontractors all win too. This required a change in thinking that really began back at Gold Canyon. We knew that people needed to understand the dire straits the company was in so they could pitch in and help come up with solutions. People needed to understand the consequences of the losing habits developed over the years and what an unhealthy environment those habits had created. They needed to realize that either we change or we won't be here; we won't have the chance to win or lose any more battles. We gave them the knowledge, and, of course, they stepped up to the challenge.

We learned that every time we raised the bar and challenged people, they ran right past it. There is an unbelievable spirit of cooperation and a habit of winning among our employees today. In Doug's words: "I was fortunate enough to be isolated in Phoenix, working for a guy who believed you should win all the time. We believed we could win while other parts of our company did not. I wanted to change the psyche around here and create a culture of winning, where losing was no longer acceptable."

Chapter 4

BACK TO BASICS

What we saw at this stage of our transition was that we wanted to become business centered as a company. We were very project centered, and everything was geared around getting the next job, sometimes without enough regard to cost. We weren't focused on the fact that Sundt was a business, and the decisions we made to get the next job had an impact on the long-term well-being of the company.

When getting the project "regardless of cost" becomes the mantra, "dumb" can become the driving force of key decisions. This was why we had to begin teaching our profit center managers about running a business, not just getting the next project. This was the beginning of getting back to the basics of running a good business. It was not an easy transition, but one that was paramount if we were going to survive. We had to address many issues simultaneously if we were going to make any progress. One of these was the issue of claims.

Although we had finally worked through most of our construction claims, we still had not made the progress needed to get this company headed in the right direction. We weren't willing to take a hard look in the mirror. We were afraid of what we might see. Many of the problems we were faced with were self-inflicted. To this day we're not exactly sure why we would not address our many problems, and maybe we will never clearly understand.

Most people really want to do a good job and contribute to the success of the organization, but quite often we don't arm them with the right information and knowledge for them to be successful. Because information was so tightly held, only a few people in the company knew how serious the problem really was. In Richard's words, "Doug had been running the Phoenix office and was also a member of the Board of Directors and even as a board member he had a limited idea of the truth of the financial mess the company had gotten itself into."

Most of the agenda for our board meetings were reports by Wilson on future opportunities, often in the international market. Board meetings did include a financial report, but it was more of a 30,000-foot-level report, and we didn't spend much time on the performance of our operating units. We did spend time on those issues that we were obligated to look at, such as our ESOP and its repurchase liabilities. Wilson wasn't comfortable with confrontation, so if any agenda item was questioned, it was usually deferred to a future meeting and never seemed to make it to the next agenda. Most other employees, however, including senior managers, were ignorant of the real financial health of the company. After Gold Canyon, all those in attendance clearly understood the magnitude of our dilemma because we had opened up our books, and from that day forward they were going to stay open. Again, this was absolutely fundamental to our turnaround as a company.

Sundt was about to go back to the drawing board of business fundamentals, and relearn all the things we had somehow forgotten about how to run a successful business. It was time to go back to the basics. One of the best things we did to get on track was to put together an outside advisory board. This board was made up of three gentlemen we knew well and had a lot of respect for. They were very active in the construction industry and brought a lot of knowledge to the table. They were also people we knew would question us if they believed that we were going down the wrong road or weren't addressing something they thought we should address. These individuals were Bill Deasy, CEO of TL James; Hugh Rice, Chairman of FMI; and Jack Lowe, CEO of TD Industries, and we owe them a great deal of gratitude for their advice and counsel. The advisory board paved the way for our decision some years later to add outside members to our board of directors. This period of time was really critical, because the situation was dire and we had no choice but to work on the most critical items. The next biggest hurdle, and in some ways our most risky, was to call a combined meeting with our bank and bonding company to advise them of the magnitude of the problems we were experiencing.

It's not easy to look the people who provide you credit and bonding in the eye and tell them that you want to write off a significant number of the claims on your balance sheet because you won't be able to collect the money.

We wanted to clean up our balance sheet and give ourselves an opportunity to start making a reasonable return on equity, which would give our employees some hope again and get their attitudes turned around. This was also a significant key to our survival.

We also knew that if the meeting didn't go well, either our bank or bonding company could put us out of business. Fortunately, Ray Bargull had a very good relationship with our banker, and I had recently developed a good relationship with our bonding company.

Both firms agreed with our plan for moving forward, let us write off the claims, and said they would stand behind us as we moved forward. When we wrote off those questionable claims, the company's net worth dropped by 20 percent. That was a tough day, but in retrospect it may have been one of the best days in my career. Sundt had now lost a third of its net worth since 1992. We had a pretty deep hole to crawl out of, but at least we still had an opportunity to become successful again. The ball was in our court, and it was our time to look to the future and stop reflecting on the past. Being a victim would not get it done.

The actions we took got us off the heart monitor, so to speak. By 1999 we were becoming healthy again and only needed weekly check-ups.

Becoming honest about our problems, making some tough choices, and starting down the road of getting back to the basics moved us away from the brink of disaster and headed toward stability. This does not mean that we immediately became perfectly healthy again, but at least we were surviving.

In Richard's words:

We started seeing tangible results of our efforts during the early part of our turnaround years, in 1998 and 1999, but had light years to go to get us where we needed to be. We had to develop consistency of performance at all of our operating units so we could improve and grow our earnings, our cash balances, pay down our debt, and start building our net worth. At that point, most of the changes were driven from the top down. That's not the best way to run a company, but for the times it was the only way. Doug maintained the title of both chairman of the board and president, and had not named a chief operating officer. There were so many changes to make and, and most were going to be very uncomfortable, so he really didn't want anyone between him and the profit center managers at this stage. He also didn't know who was the best candidate for that position and didn't want to be rushed into the decision. When a company is in critical condition and you start openly sharing information about not only your financials but also the many other problems you are experiencing, people begin to realize you are making the hard decisions needed to get things turned around, and you begin to gain back the credibility you lost.

Disciplined Execution

Somewhere along the way, Sundt put its checklist aside and said, "We've got this." And unfortunately this type of arrogance sent the company into a downward spiral.

> *When I flew with my mentor Jim Normand, I was immediately impressed with how disciplined he was. Jim would get in his airplane, take out his checklist and physically touch each instrument as he checked it off. He told me, "I learned a long time ago that you can skip things if you're in a hurry." So when I started flying on my own, I would do the same thing. It takes discipline to do things right. Getting a certain set of disciplines around all of your processes will reduce your chances of failure and increase your chance of success.*
>
> Doug

In our business, skipping the checklist and getting careless about your fundamentals can get you in serious trouble, negatively affecting your financial results (among other things such as safety and quality). If you lack discipline, the results won't be what they need to be for the company to survive and succeed. Getting back to basics is getting back to the things that matter, and good discipline tops that list.

Bob Sundt always taught us the value of discipline. Not only was Bob process driven but he was also a problem solver, which is a trait of being disciplined. Bob was also good at clearly defining the curbs and the goal line and then getting out of your way and letting you do your job. But he stayed informed enough to know what you were doing and could jump in and help if you needed it.

One thing that I have always found interesting is how people can justify not doing something or not following a procedure for the sake of getting a job, and how they claim that they are different, so this rule must have been meant for someone else. With that mindset you can get in trouble fast. We had become a very laissez-faire organization with little regard to processes or procedures. We had also developed the attitude that each group was uniquely different and should do its own thing its own way.

Sounds great, kind of like utopia, but it doesn't work. You can't run a high-risk low-margin business without a lot of discipline. Things were going to change and people weren't going to like it, but we were going to become a very disciplined organization.

To become disciplined, you have to have well-defined procedures and put mechanisms in place to make sure these procedures are being followed. Such processes were what we needed to develop, along with consistency in those processes and the training to make sure all of our employees knew what was expected of them and how to do their respective jobs. We discuss this later. We have learned that even with processes and training you have to pay constant attention to the issue of discipline. For some reason, perhaps just human nature, people incrementally start to lose discipline over time. In 2005, after several years of improved performance, we did not perform nearly as well as we had expected. We conducted a root cause analysis, which was something new for us, and found that we had slipped back into a project-centered mentality again. We were again focused on getting the job, not running our business. Our industry was experiencing significant escalation in material prices, and instead of protecting ourselves against this inflation with either escalation clauses in our contracts or contingencies in our estimates to cover such escalations, we had convinced ourselves that if we attempted to do that we might not get the project. Well, guess what? We got the project(s), and lost a lot of money on them because we didn't follow procedure. In essence, we lost our discipline.

We also found that we moved personnel from one project to another too quickly, and when you do that you lose continuity of leadership, and that generally creates problems for the project. Again we lost our discipline, and it cost us dearly. We could go on with this list of problems because we found several other causes, but, in short, what we learned was that no matter how hard you try, it is easy to fall back into the poor patterns of behavior that got you in so much trouble in the first place. We instituted more oversight of our projects, plus policies and procedures, to make sure we avoided such pitfalls in the future. One important lesson we learned from our analysis was that in several cases we had simply asked people to do too much and as a result they made some costly mistakes.

Measuring and Rewarding Performance

We put in place a series of performance measurements to essentially change behavior. The profit and service centers' performances, based on these standards, had a direct impact on bonuses. In the case of profit centers, we created separate bonus pools for each group, based upon the profits they made, but those pools could be dramatically increased or decreased based upon how well they also did on the fourteen performance measurements we used initially. We will talk more about the changes we made to the bonus system later in this chapter.

> *Establishing performance standards was one of the best things Doug did to change this organization. Prior to his leadership there really wasn't a system at all. The only metric we had was "did you make money?" and frankly that did not seem to matter either. Doug was the first CEO in the modern history of Sundt to establish a clear set of visible expectations for performance at all levels of the organization, and this was key for driving employee engagement and performance.*
>
> Richard

The initial performance measures focused on issues such as days in receivables, operating profit, work obtained, safety, employee satisfaction, customer satisfaction, and so on. We intentionally created performance standards aimed at changing the behaviors that had been causing poor performance of the company. For instance, our billing and collection process was awful, and as a result our cash flow was very poor, forcing us to borrow just to meet payroll. Once these targets were set and there was transparency given to how each profit center was doing, things started to change quickly. Our days in receivables quickly went from about sixty days down to where it resides today, hovering around our target of thirty-eight days. The attention to this one performance measure had an immediate and dramatic impact on the financial health of the company.

The performance targets for each group were shared across the company, and performance was made visible to anyone in the company who wanted to know. As you might imagine, some managers were very embarrassed by the performance of their organizations and did not like their dirty laundry exposed for anyone to see. However, this open-book approach accelerated changes in behavior and put pressure on the senior management of the company as a lot of people asked, "What are you doing about this?" when they could see what was going on. It was an important lesson for us and one that we want to share with those who read this book: the value of establishing performance targets and bringing transparency to the performance of the company. We frankly surprised ourselves as we were able to continue to raise the bar and take our performance to the next level. You can't make meaningful change if you don't know where the goal is and how the game is progressing.

Over time, the performance standards changed in two ways. First, we raised the bar in some cases, for instance, in safety. As we got better, we were not satisfied with just improving. We sought out what best-in-class performance was in areas such as safety and changed our performance standards. Secondly, as the turnaround identified other issues, we added and deleted performance measures to drive changes in behavior in those areas. It is critical to continually focus on an organization's key issues through performance measures.

Today we recognize that these performance standards were a key factor in creating the belief that we could perform with the very best companies in our industry. It's hard to put a value on believing in yourself, but it had a big impact on the success we had during the turnaround. The employee owners of Sundt today don't need someone at the top holding them accountable anymore. Instead they are holding themselves accountable for meeting or exceeding these standards of performance, which are benchmarked at best-in-class levels. While we did not know it at the time, performance standards addressed one of the two common characteristics of human behavior: What gets measured gets done.

The other characteristic of human behavior is that what gets rewarded also gets done. That is why probably, more out of frustration than wisdom, we tied our bonus system to these performance standards.

In Doug's words:

I can remember the day before I became CEO that I was given an envelope of bonus checks to take to a division manager so he could distribute them to employees. I asked why they were getting any kind of bonus since they had just lost several million dollars. The response was, "We are all in this together." Back then the philosophy was that if the company made money, everyone was entitled to a bonus.

There were two very disturbing trends that this kind of a reward system generated. First, there were people at Sundt who saw no connection between getting a bonus and their profit center's, or service center's, performance because frankly there was none. Second, and equally problematic, was that some managers misrepresented their performance in order to generate a bonus pool.

This behavior was characteristic of some of the subtle issues that were tearing at the values of the company and eating away at our performance. We promised ourselves that from that day forward we would only be paying bonuses for performance. So Richard was given the task of designing a new bonus system that rewarded performance and was affected by the performance measures that we were putting in place.

While Richard was working on a new design for the bonus system, Kevin Burnett, the company controller, was hard at work preparing reports and conducting audits

to ensure we could validate exactly what the performance was on a particular job. This later became known as the monthly project report (MPR), which today provides a comprehensive look at each of our projects every month.

The new bonus program had several important characteristics:

1. A profit floor for the corporation was established that had to be met before any bonuses were made.

2. Profit centers had to make a profit, or there was no bonus distribution to those employees

3.   Seventy-five percent of an individual's bonus was based upon the performance of the center they were in, and 25 percent was based upon the average performance of all the profit centers.

4.   Once the bonus pool was calculated for a profit or service center, it was adjusted up or down, based on the performance standards.

5.   Bonuses were paid twice a year. The first bonus was paid after the first six months of operation, and the second at the end of the fiscal year.

These changes were not met with a lot of enthusiasm, but they gave us a performance-based bonus system, and it was amazing how the combination of this new system and the performance standards quickly drove changes in behavior. Clearly people tend to do what gets measured and rewarded!

Managing G &A Cost

There is a saying in the construction business that "a bad job will hurt you, but overhead will kill you." Before the turnaround most employees made no connection between what it cost to run our *entire* business and making a profit. The profit centers had their own overhead budgets that had to be covered and they were measured on their operating profits. Most profit-center employees had no understanding that there was still a significant overhead cost at the corporate level that also needed to be covered if the company was to make a profit. We often heard how well a division was doing, and yes, if you looked at the individual jobs, they were making their project cost, covering their division overhead, and making a profit at the division level. But they weren't making enough profit to pay for their share of corporate overhead so the company could make a profit.

In their defense, they didn't know what their share of the corporate overhead was because it was never allocated to them and they were only responsible for their direct overhead. Saying this another way, when we allocated the corporate overhead to a division that had been showing an operating profit for the past ten years, that division often actually lost money.

We made the decision that part of the process of becoming business- centered rather than project- centered was that each profit center needed to be charged for its share of corporate overhead, and it needed to cover those costs and be measured that way. You can imagine how that went over. Interestingly the discussion centered around the question, "If we do this, how can we compete?" and the belief, "If we do this, we will go broke." Hard to believe, but it was difficult for employees to see that if we didn't start doing this, we were going to go broke anyway.

It's not an easy task to fairly allocate all of the corporate overhead to the operating units, but we did come up with a formula that satisfied (with a fair amount of kicking and screaming) all of the profit center managers. It was hard to swallow because it was such a change in the way things had been done, and I have to give the managers a lot of credit. Although they weren't happy, they intuitively knew it had to be done. They rolled up their sleeves, got on with the program, and made it work.

At corporate, we had to make sure that our overhead costs were competitive and that we weren't being foolish on how we were spending money. We had a responsibility to make sure that our costs and charges to each profit center were fair. We had to look for ways to have the most impact with the service side of our business as well. Overhead today is still an issue. There is always the argument of whether it is a cost or an investment. Should we follow the "work-one-man-short" rule, or invest in a new person or piece of equipment that might help us penetrate a new market? That will always be the debate and that's not all bad. If we are having that discussion and holding ourselves accountable for the outcome of such a decision, we will probably be able to keep things in balance and be a lot more successful as a company.

Concurrent with getting back to the basics of running a business, becoming more disciplined, creating a system that rewarded performance, and managing our overhead cost, we also knew we had a lot of additional work to do to become a better company. We had no liquidity, were very reactionary, were not strategic, weren't willing to invest in our people or technology, had a lot of nonperforming assets, and the list went on.

Cash Management

We were essentially out of cash and continuing to borrow to finance our operation. Again, the lack of discipline was coming into play. We were not billing our projects accurately or in a timely fashion, and we weren't collecting our money. In essence, we were financing our customers' projects interest free. Not a very good business strategy.

In the weeks following Gold Canyon, we really focused on our cash management, and our cash balances began to improve. But just as quickly, our lack of discipline kicked in again. We soon reverted to old habits, and our cash position sunk to the same levels as before. It was about this time that Sundt hired Kevin Burnett as our comptroller, and he deserves a lot of credit for correcting some very poor cash management habits.

Kevin put into place processes that would improve timeliness of billing and collections. When a job wasn't billed accurately and on time, the profit center manager would get an email from Kevin, wanting an answer immediately as to why that was the case. If we didn't receive a check on the day it was contractually due, Kevin was on the phone with the profit center manager, and they, in turn, would be in contact with the customer, wanting to know when we were going to get paid.

In Doug's words:

"I recall getting complaints from a lot of the profit center managers about Kevin and how he was a real pain in the butt. My pat answer was, "If you don't like it, start billing and collecting on time, and you won't hear from him. If you can't do that, he will continue to be a pain in the butt, and he has my permission to be one.""

Kevin also set up goals for days in receivables, aged receivables, cash as a percentage of equity, and so on; we started measuring performance by those goals. The failure to meet those goals had an impact on the profit center's bonus pool. Another of Kevin's pet projects was to improve our payables as we improved our receivables. Getting our subcontractors paid in a timely fashion is very important, and as we got better at collections, we wanted them to benefit as well.

As we began to improve our cash balances, we put a schedule in place to pay down our debt that in 1998 was 120 percent of our net worth. We became debt free in 2002 and haven't borrowed a nickel since. Today we have a very strong balance sheet with a significant cash balance.

What puts us in the position we are in today versus where we were in 1998 is the ability to invest in our future and grow our business. We have the ability to invest in talent, technology, training, and other lines of business or assets that can earn a decent return so we aren't as reliant on construction profits alone. I think everyone understands the importance of keeping our cash balances up and managing the financial strength of our organization. Ray Bargull, our CFO, initially hired Kevin in hopes that Kevin would succeed him once he retired, and Kevin did not disappoint us. By 2000 we had made significant progress in all of these areas while teaching people the simple lesson that cash management is a critical business basic that cannot be ignored without serious consequences.

Kevin was instrumental in rebuilding the balance sheet, improving our cash balances, and paying down our debt. The flywheel effect Jim Collins explains in his book Good to Great is working very well for us today in the area of cash management, and the process has taken on a life of its own. People get it. They understand the importance of cash management, and they have become very disciplined at making sure their jobs are billed accurately and on time, and that we collect what we are due in a timely fashion. Without Kevin's incredible discipline and willingness to do what needed to be done to right what was wrong about cash management, the turnaround would have been longer and more taxing.

We had become more disciplined and had started to manage our cash flow. This isn't something profound or some innovative idea! It is basic to managing a good company. We were successfully making the journey back to the basics of business, and now we had to focus on taking this company to a new level of performance. Over the next few years we would really have to focus on the key issues listed below if we were going to successfully turn this company around and build the platform for its sustainability. What we were beginning to embark on wasn't rocket science or some silver bullet that would be a quick fix; it was just common sense. Unfortunately, for whatever reason, we weren't doing these things and they weren't part of our DNA as a company. This wasn't just about getting off life support; it was about developing processes in a company that should have been there but weren't, and institutionalizing the discipline so we could obtain consistency in our performance.

As we worked through these issues they became part of what we were attempting to become as a company so we could eventually focus on growth, which we discuss later in the book.

- Strategic Planning

- People Development

- Succession Planning

- Technology/Innovation

- Asset Management

- Organizational Consistency

This was also a time to energize the tremendous talent at Sundt and get that talent actively engaged in helping us address these issues, raise the bar, and change the company in a very impactful way. In other words, we wanted what we were going to embark on to become part of the Sundt DNA so the company could be sustained for future generations of employee owners.

We assembled committees of talented Sundt employees and brought in outside talent, when appropriate, to begin addressing these critical areas of a turnaround.

Building Blocks

1) The company had become very project centered and not focused on running a business. It became critical to teach profit center managers how to run a business and how to understand the true costs of running

a business. It was also important to share more and better information about the company's performance with those who could impact it.

a) Do your managers and your employees understand the basic principles of business and accounting?

b) Do your managers and employees have access to information about the company's performance, including financial performance?

c) Do you have good systems in place to accurately track performance?

2) In 1992 the company was mired in a large number of claims and it was clear that the only way to move forward was to write off a significant amount of money. This was a risky proposition as Sundt's bank and bonding company could have closed the company. But based on the company's excellent reputation and long relationship with those two companies they were able to do that and begin crawling out of a very deep hole.

a) Do you have past sins that you simply need to let go of and move forward?

b) Have you been honest with your bank or other financial organizations about your situation and built a good relationship with those individuals?

c) Are you willing to take the risk to quit digging a deeper hole and start working your way out of the hole?

3) Sundt had historically rewarded all divisions and employees with bonuses, even when a division lost money or the company's performance did not warrant it. One of the significant and unpopular decisions that Doug made was to tie division bonuses to a set of performance measurements and not award bonuses to any employee in a division that did not make money. The bonus system was designed to reward the "upstream" efforts that led to profitability, including financial management, safety, and employee development.

a) Does your company tie bonuses or compensation to performance in some manner?

b) Does your company's system of compensation (and bonuses) provide the appropriate incentives to managers and employees to improve performance?

c) What gets measured gets done. Are you measuring the right things?

Chapter 5

STRATEGIC PLANNING AND MANAGEMENT

In the years before Gold Canyon we were largely a "silo-driven" company, meaning that people were doing their own thing most of the time, and there was very little organizational consistency. We didn't have a common sense of where the company was headed, or an understanding of our vision, mission, and so on. And we certainly didn't know how to get ourselves out of the mess we were in.

In Richard's words:

Planning at Sundt had been nearly nonexistent, at least corporately. We were simply an opportunistic company, pursuing and building construction projects with little thought about risk, profit potential, etc. There was no context for decision making. It became clear that we needed a plan and a way of communicating it if we were going to pull away from the abyss and prosper.

We determined that we needed to have a strategic plan for the organization, but we really were not sure what that meant. The manager of our Sacramento office, Bob Earl, was teaching some classes at Sacramento State University on strategic management, based upon the model developed by Steve Haines, founder of the Haines Center for Strategic Management in San Diego, California. Since we already had somewhat of a relationship with Steve, it seemed logical to contact him for help in this area. We had the wisdom to know what we didn't know and seek out someone to help us.

We could probably write a book on this issue alone and the importance it played in turning around the company, but that is not the purpose here. We do, however, want to elaborate on some of the key things we learned from Steve about the process and how strategic planning and management contributed to our turnaround.

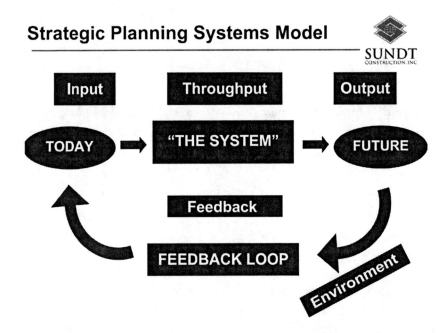

There are a lot of consultants in the area of strategic planning, and we were fortunate to end up with Steve. Steve's planning model has two important components that I think differentiate it from other planning processes we have seen. First, it is a "systems" model. What is important about systems is that all of the parts interact. That is true of this planning model. You have to engage all the components of the model and realize that they are not independent of each other. Second, and most important, is that Steve's planning model starts with the end in mind. A lot of planning can be summed up this way: First you identify something you think needs doing, and then you start brainstorming activities that you hope will end up achieving whatever it is you wanted to accomplish. We learned early on the value of trying to clearly identify where you want to go (future state) first, followed by some key measures that will help you know if you have arrived. Next, take an honest look at where you are today and then identify the key bridging strategies that will get you from where you are now to where you want to be. Then ensure at each step that you are considering the environment in which the organization finds itself. This is Steve's model, and it has served us well.

There are a couple of other things that we learned along the way as we became more engaged with this planning model. First came the notion of organizational consistency and operational flexibility. We have come to understand that this is at play in many other things in the business besides planning. The things that you want all parts of the company to do the same way are the organizationally consistent items. Operational flexibility comes into play if you don't care whether or not the policy, procedure, best practice, and so on is done the same way across the entire company. This balance is almost always at play as you make decisions. In the case of strategic planning, for instance, we wanted organizational consistency around the company vision, mission, core values, and the key bridging strategies that would get us to our ideal future state. However, the specific tactics that profit and service centers would use to achieve those strategies were left to those organizations to figure out. Too much organizational consistency turns a company into a bureaucratic nightmare and stifles innovation. Too much operational flexibility creates confusion, inefficiencies, and silos. In the years immediately following Gold Canyon, our scale was weighted heavily toward organizational consistency. We really had a low-trust environment for a while, but as we improved our training, the curbs moved further apart, and today we have good blend of these components.

Through our early mentoring by Steve and his folks we became aware of Harvard University's balanced scorecard process. What made sense to us was that there are four big areas you need to pay attention to in any business: your people, your business processes, your customers, and financial management. This simplistic look at the scorecard has served us well as today we believe that if you have the right people, in the right roles, working with a continually improved business process, all of which are focused on your customer, good financial performance will follow. We had been focused on profits, had not done too well at making any, and had lost sight of the means to that end. As a side note, we have found this notion of looking for the means to an end applies in many instances. Another example of this is given in the chapter on business development.

We have become pretty good planners and continue to improve on the really important point of managing by the plan. Your plans should be the context in which decisions are made. However they are not strait jackets. For example, the tragedy of 9/11/2001 rendered almost all company plans invalid, to a large degree, by the following day. We redid our plans in reaction to that event, and have had to do so again several other times in reaction to market changes.

We were lucky in this area as a few of our profit center managers embraced the process, thinking it would improve their business performance, and it did. Those early adopters helped jump start the rest of the organization. However, Doug had already made it clear that everyone was going to participate in managing the company strategically. One final and very important outcome of this planning process, which we mentioned early but is worth repeating, is that strategic planning helped rid our culture of its destructive silo mentality. We are one company now, all pulling in the same direction, and that is a powerful force.

Before we leave the topic of strategic planning and management there is one other related and important issue that needs to be discussed. In the ideal future component of the planning model Steve taught us, we chose to include another concept from Jim Collins's book *Built to Last*: the BHAG, or big, hairy, audacious goal.

The book's researchers noted that the successful companies they studied, in almost all cases, had a big goal established by the head of the company that would challenge the organization. Sundt was in need of such a goal, and as part of the first strategic planning process, Doug established the first Sundt BHAG, which was to be a $1 billion company with a net worth of $100 million in ten years. Our first BHAG was 1-100-10.

As Doug explains it:

I sat down with our controller, Kevin Burnett, and said, "We need a target on the wall that everyone can visually see that clearly states where we're going." That target became 1-100-10. There was immediate resistance to the 1-100-10 target. It was pointed out to us on numerous occasions that nothing in Sundt's history would indicate that we could ever perform in a way that would allow us to meet this goal. We were talking about quadrupling our net worth in ten years. People would stare at us incredulously and ask, "*How* are we going to do this?" My answer was that I didn't have a clue, but believed it was doable and now it was our job to figure out how we could get it done. The goal was more than just a financial target; it was an essential part of us getting better as a company. We needed to have a very visible vision of where we wanted to go. In the old days we simply didn't have a vision of success.

As we began to think about how we would accomplish this goal, it was decided that we would have to sit down and define what things might look like in ten years, for our company, our industry, the economy, and other aspects of the world that impact what we do. Then, we would need to back up from 2008 to 1998 and begin reshaping the company in order to get there successfully. This idea of working backwards to identify the interim steps that would need to be implemented to achieve a goal was, in hindsight, one of the best things we did. You can't change an organization in the last year of a ten-year plan, but you can make significant changes each year by systematically executing the changes needed to attain the end goal.

Out of this process came the first ten-year plan. At the end of each year, we would "true up" the year, replacing projected numbers with actual ones and adding a year to the end of the cycle. The process of developing this first ten-year plan raised a number of questions, most notably, "What will 2008 look like?" For example, we predicted that a recession was inevitable, based on the

economy at the time. You can't go up, up, up forever. It was not a matter of
if, but when, things would come falling down. Again, in hindsight, projecting
your mind ahead ten years and being honest about the potential for a recession
and its impact on such a cyclical industry really turned out to be an important
aspect of our plan. We initially picked 2007–8 as recession years, but later
revised the period to 2008–2009. With this fundamental factor built into the
plan, it was time to think about how a recession would impact the company.

Kevin Burnett and I have a keen interest in the economy and follow different
periodicals and economic reports to make the best informed predictions we
can; we are both news freaks. I think this is an area that a lot of middle-market
companies fail at. We have also learned to follow our gut at times and this has
served us well.

The world doesn't automatically come to an end with a recession. Each
industry is uniquely affected. In construction, housing usually leads the way
into a recession. Since Sundt doesn't construct housing, that would not be an
issue in our 1998–2008 plan. When the housing market suffers, there is a chain
reaction that affects retail and commercial building. Again, this wasn't a huge
issue for us because we don't do much work in those sectors. However, the chain
reaction continues when the private sector becomes nervous about the direction
of the economy and starts to cut back. That posed a real problem for us at the
time, because 85 percent of our work was for the private sector, and 15 percent
was for the public sector.

*Problem #1: We were heavily weighted in the private
sector, which would be a dangerous financial problem
for us if private sector cut backs played out.*

Next, we looked at who spends the money in a recession. The federal
government does to stimulate the economy through a host of government,
military, and administrative programs.

Problem #2: Our federal division was in shambles.

Who else spends money during a recession? State and local governments, in conjunction with the federal government, are called upon for road, highway, bridge, and utility work. Before the term *shovel ready* was popular, we needed to make sure that we were.

Problem #3: Our highway division was in disarray.

Also in a recession, money will be spent on infrastructure projects, such as sewage treatment, water treatment, and pipelines.

Problem #4: We had just shut down our industrial division.

If we believed our own predictions about a recession in 2008–2009, we were going to have a difficult time surviving the downturn, let alone be able take advantage of the opportunities that would exist. If 1-100-10 was a real and meaningful goal for us, it was time to alter our entire organization, and not in a subtle way, as Doug explains:

At the time, 1-100-10 seemed like a very steep hill to climb, and most didn't think we had a chance of getting there. Much to the surprise of those naysayers we blew right by our initial BHAG, so we increased it again, and again, and again. The BHAG concept helped us believe in ourselves, and the process that Kevin and I went through to establish that first ten-year plan proved to be invaluable. It was our first, honest assessment at what might happen during that time, and forced us to look backwards at what we needed to work on if we were going to meet our goal.

Today our work is split about 85 public and 15 percent private and the lion's share of our profits have come from what used to be our dysfunctional federal and highway divisions and a newly formed industrial division. As we begin to look at the next ten years, we will continue to shift the organization to be prepared to compete and sustain our profitability as our economy continues to ebb and flow.

The Sundt Way

Organizational Consistency and Operational Flexibility

We talked about organizational consistency and operational flexibility in the strategic planning and management chapter, but an important part of the turnaround was what we now call the Sundt Way. The Sundt Way is the name we give to the organizationally consistent policies and procedures that we expect to be followed by all parts of the company.

We had made several key hires with experience in other construction companies and they were amazed at the lack of procedural documentation and consistency in operational processes at Sundt. Their experience as superintendents or project managers had been to be handed a set of manuals with instructions to read and understand because "that is how we do things here." Not so at Sundt. If you were lucky, someone took you under his wing and let you know how things "really" got done, but as people moved from one part of the company to another, they often found that the same procedure was done completely differently in different divisions. We had something like fifteen time sheets in the company and you can imagine how productive that was for our payroll department.

To say the least, the Sundt Way was not initially met with a whole lot of enthusiasm. Various parts of the company had gotten used to doing it "their" way and were not too pleased with the idea that we were all going to do it the Sundt Way. In the end, our people understood the horrible inefficiencies we were experiencing as a result of a "siloed" culture and the legal and financial risks involved in this kind of approach to managing the company.

Trust was low in the company in the years immediately following Gold Canyon and for good reason, but it was in that environment that the Sundt Way was created, and as a result, we developed a lot of procedures, policies, and so on. We developed manuals for the estimating and operations parts of the business, safety, and administration. This was in large part a very good process and it showed clearly how fragmented our processes were. But, over time, the

Sundt Way continued to grow and we seemed to become obsessed with making sure every little process was turned into a procedure; we were in real danger of becoming too bureaucratic and stifling innovation. We found ourselves developing a policy in reaction to the poor decisions of a small number of people. Learn from us the importance of keeping things in perspective and don't let the organizational consistency side of the scale get out of balance.

Today we enjoy a much higher level of trust resulting from the investment we have made in the development of our people, our improved performance, and some hard decisions on accountability that sent some of our people packing. As a result, we are becoming less bureaucratic. However, we do work for the federal government and the compliance involved with that kind of work has driven the need to expand our policies and procedures as the penalties for making a mistake, intended or not, are great.

Building Blocks

1) In a manner consistent with the company's traditional silo mentality, there had never been a concerted effort for corporate strategic planning. Sundt adopted a model from Steve Haines that focused on strategic "management", not just planning, and that model and process continues to be one of the keys to our success.

    a) Does your organization have a good model and process for strategic and tactical planning?

    b) Do you create plans to collect dust on a shelf, or do you use those plans to actively manage your business and guide your decisions?

    c) Are you willing to adapt your plan when the environment changes (e.g., 9/11)?

2) Striking an appropriate balance between organizational consistency and operational flexibility is both important and difficult. Too little consistency creates conflict and inefficiencies, while too much consistency can create bureaucracy and stifle innovation. Early in the transition we forced more consistency, and today we are backing off to allow for increased innovation.

   a) Does your company have an appropriate set of organizational policies and procedures and do employees follow them?

   b) Do you avoid the practice of creating new policies or procedures to solve the transgressions of one or two individuals?

   c) Do you have a process for periodically reviewing policies and procedures to make sure they are current and necessary?

3) One of the components of the first corporate strategic plan in 1998 was the BHAG (big, hairy, audacious goal) of 1-100-10. Although most managers and employees thought it was completely unrealistic, we achieved it ahead of schedule and have done the same with every subsequent goal.

   a) Does your organization have a BHAG or some highly inspirational goal that everyone can strive to achieve?

   b) Do you regularly report to managers and employees on your progress in reaching the BHAG?

   c) Do employees have a line of sight to your BHAG and/or company goals?

Chapter 6

BECOMING
A LEARNING
ORGANIZATION

"Doug had made a proposal to the board of directors in the late '80s about establishment of a significant training program at Sundt, which basically fell on deaf ears. There had been some efforts to do training before, but when things got tough, we, like many companies in this industry, would shut our training programs down. Essentially the company had not been willing to invest in its future by investing in its employees, something he wanted to change when he had the opportunity and the position to make it happen.

In 1993, when I was brought in to do craft training, we were starting to get serious about requiring specific training for certain types of jobs. In 1996 after the Gold Canyon retreat, we started to ramp up the training of all of our employees, and that's when training really started to take root as part of the company culture."

Richard

Part of what surfaced when we were looking at the many problems we were experiencing was the fact that many of our people who may have been well educated and well intentioned still lacked training in some of the basic fundamentals related to their specific job. There were some significant discussions with our human resources people at Gold Canyon that raised some big questions for us.

For instance, what set of skills did our people need to properly and consistently execute their jobs so Sundt could become more successful? This could be anything from properly abstracting subcontractor quotations, writing subcontracts, scheduling a project, procurement management, change manage, cash management, project closeout, and a host of other important processes. As we started to develop our first strategic plan, we also wanted our training efforts to support the strategies identified in our plan.

As a result, we started to invest a lot more in our people over the next couple years, providing more of a broad-based developmental foundation, which our people needed to do their jobs well. In a business like ours people can come from another company with a different way of doing things. Absent a clear, well-established, articulated Sundt way of doing things, they are going to keep doing it their way. Investing in our people meant giving them the tools and resources they needed to understand the Sundt Way and be successful in doing their jobs.

Richard explains how they came up with development models:

One of the best things I did at Sundt was fire the previous training director (myself) and hire Dave Muehlbauer. Dave was a fellow educator with me at the Arizona Department of Education. While I'm more of a big-picture guy, Dave is an analyzer and is better at getting things organized and in doing so getting things done. He has taken us places I never would have been able to.

Shortly after Dave joined Sundt, we held a meeting in Prescott, Arizona (a small community north of Phoenix). Just the two of us were present, and the result was creation of two development models that have served as the foundation for our training and development program over the years. The first pyramid model illustrates that we are providing training to all individuals in the organization including our craft workforce and shows that skill needs change as people advance upward in the pyramid. The pyramid also illustrates with the arrows at each level the important notion that as you move up, you start to look outside your own job and at some point even outside the company.

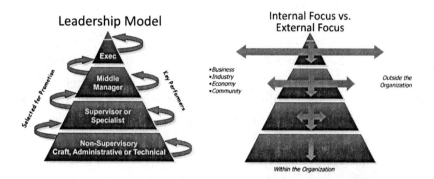

The second illustration describes the kinds of skills needed by individuals as they move from entry-level positions up to senior management positions. These two simple diagrams have served as the foundation for our training efforts for many years now, and we have shared them widely with others in our industry.

Dave Muehlbauer then developed a set of core competencies that by definition are the common set of knowledge and skills needed by all the employee-owners of Sundt. However, the level of skill needed can vary widely depending on the position you hold in the company. One of the core competencies is oral communication. The levels of oral communication competence we expect from a field engineer and a profit center manager are very different and this is the reason we developed competency indicators for each competency at each level in the pyramid model. Some years later, we developed the technical competencies associated with the specific responsibilities of a large number of positions.

These competencies serve as the content focus for the classes and academies that we offer. The company's willingness to take the risk of hiring a couple of educators has been instrumental in developing what we—with a high degree of bias—think is one of the best training programs in the industry.

With these items in place we had established the basic infrastructure for Sundt to becoming a learning organization. By investing in our people and making sure they had the right skill sets for the job, we were sowing the seeds of leadership for the future. We have conducted training not only for our employee-owners but also for subcontractors, owners, and other contractors. Consistent with our core values, we are committed to bettering our industry when we have a chance to do so.

As we transitioned from survival to a long-term sustainability mode, investing in our future has become a lasting piece of our infrastructure. From those humble beginnings, today Sundt has a very robust, award-winning, and nationally recognized training program. We made it a point to invest in developing all of our people rather than focusing on a few at the top, hoping that knowledge and attitude toward training would trickle down magically throughout the organization. Education doesn't work that way and we knew it. Therefore our training program from the very beginning included executives, middle managers, supervisors, our craft work force, administrative personnel, and everyone in between. The new paradigm was that, whether you are a clerk or the CEO, there is training for you at Sundt.

In hindsight, it has been clear that working to improve the skill sets of all the people in the organization was a critical centerpiece of our investment in becoming a learning organization.

If you come to Sundt today, you will indeed find a very robust set of development programs delivered by our own people and outside experts. About 10 percent of our training content is delivered online, and we are growing that percentage to make access easier, especially for those who are project based. Not all training is suited to online delivery, but where it makes sense, we want to do more of it.

We have required classes and some that must be completed in the first ninety days of employment so folks can become productive as soon as possible. We sponsor two craft apprenticeship programs and offer numerous ad hoc classes for our craft employee-owners.

A lot of our delivery is through our Sundt Academies. We have academies for leadership, project managers, project superintendents, estimators, marketing, engineers, and estimators. The academies have proven to be an effective way of insuring organizational consistency across the company in the duties associated with these positions and in the communicating strategic initiatives we are pursuing in the near future and increasing alignment throughout the teams across multiple domains.

Another part of our training and development program has been tuition reimbursement. We support the higher education goals of our employee owners including our craft workers when they demonstrate that the education will either improve their ability to perform their present job and/or prepare them for the next position on their career ladder. We are proud of the large number of employees who have earned their bachelor's or master's degrees, paid for by the company.

Somewhat related is our internship program. We learned some years ago that showing up to recruit at colleges and universities on career days in competition with ten of our best competitors was very unproductive. Therefore we now have most of our entry-level employees in engineering serve one or more years of internship with us. They get to know us and we get to know them, and both parties tend to make a better decision about employment at Sundt. The company also provides scholarships for select interns during their final year of schooling.

In the next chapter some special attention will be given to our leadership development programs and succession planning, which was the catalyst for those programs. The important thing to take away from this part of the book is that our investment in the development of our people is one of the major contributors to the success of the turnaround at Sundt.

Building Blocks

1) The company had resisted investing in training and development until Doug was in a position to implement it. Clearly, we had a lot of employees with good educations and good intentions but without a clear understanding of the basic expectations of their job. Establishing a training organization was an important part of our transformation.

   a) Does your company have an effective program of training and development for your employees?

   b) Is your company's training and development program tied to your strategic plan and priorities?

   c) Are company leaders involved in the training program, providing guidance and support, and participating themselves?

2) In the early days of the company's training program we created a comprehensive model for the program that was shared with and accepted by the senior leadership of the company. That model persists today and continues to drive the company's training program.

   a) Have you taken the time to carefully understand what you expect your company's training and development program to accomplish?

   b) Does your company's training and development program take advantage of the best thinking in the industry and incorporate current research and practices?

   c) Do you have the involvement of employees and managers in continually improving the company's training and development program?

3) One of the other intentional characteristics of the training and development program at Sundt was that all employees would be involved, not just a select few. The company provides training opportunities from the CEO to the craft worker. This approach assures that each employee has the right skill sets for the job, and supports career development and advancement.

   a) Is your company's training and development program comprehensive in nature and do you provide something for everyone?

   b) Do your company's training programs serve both the current job skill needs of employees and longer-term career development needs?

   c) Are employees and their supervisors directly involved in identifying the employee's training needs and are supervisors held accountable for the employee's development?

M.M. Sundt

Agua Pura Dam – 1911

Methodist Church – 1929

Las Alamos –1943

Stanford Linear Accelerator, Beam Switchyard – 1964

Apollo Launch Pad – 1965

Tempe Municipal Building – 1970

Upper Mahaio Power Plant Philippines – 1996

London Bridge – 1972

Cripple Creek Gold Mine – 1995

Great Western Bank – 1975

Cyprus Sierrita Open Pit – 1975

Reunion Tower –1976

US Bank – 1978

Ventana Canyon Resort – 1983

Salt River Project Corporate Headquarters – 1986

Unisource Tower – 1986

Arizona Canal Diversion Channel – 1991

Papago Expressway – 1991

Holnman Devil's Slide, Preheater Tower – 1998

Austin Bergstrom Airport – 1998

US Embassy – Moscow – 1999

US60 – Design/Build Widening Project – 2003

Air Force Academy – 2003

Edinburg Border Station – 2004

Seaworld Journey to Atlantis – 2004

Sony – 2006

ASU Biodesign Exterior – 2007

ASU Walter Cronkite School of Journalism – 2008

Loop 202 – 2010

Tucson Electric Power Coal Conversion – 1986

Dial – 2011

LEAP 3.1 June 2007

LEAP CEO Forum

Strategic Planning

START CEO Forum

START Team Building Activity

Chapter 7

SECURING
OUR FUTURE

Providing for the Orderly Succession and Development of Leadership

"The push for training, education, employee development, and succession planning started because Doug didn't receive formal training for any of the jobs he held at Sundt, and the other areas were simply not priorities for the company. This is a macho industry that historically didn't see the need to invest in its people. They either got it done or you ran them off. As president, Doug immediately said, 'We're not going to have any more of that kind of thinking at Sundt.'

Initially Doug was pretty "top down" in managing the company. But that was not going to work for very long, and we knew we had to make a serious commitment to developing the future leadership of the company. These new leaders would need to have a keen sense of the values of the company because this issue had caused a very successful company to nearly fail. They would also need the skills to take the company to places the current leadership could not even imagine."

Richard

Actually, we had started just prior to Gold Canyon to involve the top leadership of the company in a well-recognized leadership development program offered by the Center for Creative Leadership. These weeklong sessions had approximately twenty-five participants. In most cases they were from a variety of companies. There were a lot of assessments done prior to and during the sessions, and the feedback from those assessments was usually the highlight of the week, although in many cases the participants got, for the first time, some frank feedback on issues affecting their leadership ability. For those of us who participated there were a couple of outcomes that impacted the leadership development programs we have now institutionalized at Sundt. First, the unanimous feedback from the Sundt folks was that they would have benefited from this type of experience much earlier in their careers. We also learned that the current leadership pretty much saw the world the same way, and that was probably not a good thing. As a result, we formed corporate committees that helped improve the diversity of people involved in finding solutions to our problems. There is a great video, produced some years ago by Joel Barker, on the relationship between diversity, innovation, and wealth. The bottom line of that video is the undeniable value, in terms of innovation, that comes from involving people who have a diverse set of experiences, personalities, and so on.

Another issue came up that brought some urgency to the development of our leadership programs, and that was the initiative to look at a performance-based, long-term incentive plan for key leaders in the company. What we found was that within a very small window of time, most of the senior executives would be retiring, and we really had not developed the next generation of leaders to take their place. As a result we recognized the need to get serious about succession planning.

In April 1996, just as we were developing Sundt's first succession planning activities, the importance of what we were doing was driven home by a tragedy that made international headlines. While on a trade mission, an aircraft carrying U.S. Commerce Secretary Ron Brown and thirty-four others crashed into a mountainside in Croatia, killing everyone on board. Also lost in the crash were several construction industry executives whose organizations subsequently fell into shambles without their leadership.

Five years later this story would be repeated on 9/11. When the towers went down, several companies lost their entire leadership team, and many of those companies were not around two years later.

Chrysler chairman Lee Iacocca, iconic for the company turnaround he orchestrated, is a great example of how important it is for current management to prepare the next crop of leaders to take a healthy company into future prosperity. He put nobody between him and the problems at hand. That style of direct management may have been required to fix Chrysler at the time. Yet that same style resulted in the company having no one prepared to sustain the organization after Iacocca left the company.

Without succession planning strategies, companies are putting themselves at risk for the desperate now-what-do-we-do? scenarios described above. It was no different at Sundt in 1992 when Doug found himself at the helm of a company with no succession strategies beyond giving someone else the wheel and hoping for the best. We wanted to ensure that when we left the transition to new leadership would be well planned and communicated years prior to our official exit so that success and growth could continue uninterrupted.

One of the primary functions of training and education is to ensure the orderly succession of people within a company. Recall from earlier in this book the reaction of the board of directors when Doug presented the idea of investing money in training; they turned it down. By the 1990s, without a comprehensive training and education program in place, Sundt was lacking any clear strategies for succession.

Our entire organization was full of very qualified managers who were retiring and had failed to prepare those who would follow them to successfully lead their respective divisions. Consequently we suffered significant losses. This was certainly a poor method of planning for a successful future. One of our top priorities during the turnaround years was to create clear succession plans and exit strategies in order to develop future leaders in all of our divisions.

We initiated many development strategies to accomplish these goals, but our Leadership Excellence Accelerates Performance (LEAP) program exceeded all of our expectations. LEAP takes individuals at the middle management level and develops them as future leaders. The program typically has twenty participants, selected and approved by division and corporate management.

The focus of the LEAP program is threefold:

1. Increase business and management skills as they apply to Sundt Construction

2. Enhance the leadership and teamwork skills of participants

3. Encourage and increase collaboration

LEAP is a three-year program, with seven three-day sessions (six months apart). The first session provides the overview and focuses on self-awareness. The second session is a significant leadership and team-building experience. The remaining sessions cover the three aspects of our business (business development, preconstruction and operations) in detail, plus selected business and leadership competencies.

Between the group sessions, there are selected team projects and activities occurring among participants. These projects have addressed significant issues facing the company, and the findings from the LEAP teams have had a major positive impact on the company. Also included in LEAP, and in alignment with the company's core values, is a required community service experience.

The staffing for LEAP was the two of us as well as David Muehlbauer and Bob Petrello. We don't think any of us missed more than one part of a session in the first LEAP class, and that commitment holds true today.

In Richard's words:

Doug made it apparent from his presence the importance we were placing on developing the next generation of leaders. Bob played the key role in planning and executing the team building activities at each session and also chose the various assessment instruments that we used over the duration of the program. One other program component worth mentioning is the CEO Forum. During each session, Doug conducts a 90-minute Q & A session with the participants. The participants have direct access to the top leader of the company, and can ask him anything they want. At times Doug uses these forums to present specific topics and then engages the participants in discussions about them.

Prior to LEAP, the person who replaced a division leader when he or she retired was typically a loyal employee who was simply promoted without being adequately trained to run a business unit. It was a fly-by-the-seat-of-their pants experience, and while they succeeded in some limited cases, most failed. This was the company's fault, not the employee's. We failed them; they didn't necessarily fail us. We paid a huge price for our failure to have a formal, successful succession program. Today, thanks to LEAP, the company enjoys the benefits of a much more developed group of people who are bringing the entire organization to a higher level due to their experiences in this program.

One of the more important things about LEAP is that while we knew we needed to do something, we were not quite sure what. Fortunately we had the courage to try, and in this case the results exceeded our wildest expectations. Today over 50 percent of the senior management of the company are LEAP graduates.

The most remarkable thing about LEAP is that we took a chance and tried it—and it worked! This is a huge differentiator from other companies, which, when they reach the edge of the abyss, cower in fear, taking small, conservative steps to survive. Realistically speaking, most companies in a crisis mode are not eager to take risks, financial or otherwise. It is really not funny, but often we have observed in our company and in others that when things get tough, the leaders of the organization revert to the ways of the past, and in doing so just starting digging the hole they're in deeper and faster. This can also be seen in the following illustration, Life Cycle of a Company. If you get over on the right side of the curve, where Sundt was, you can die quickly.

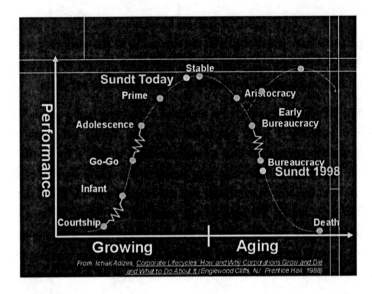

From Ichak Adizes, *Corporate Lifecycles: How and Why Corporations Grow and Die and What to Do About It* (Englewood Cliffs, NJ: Prentice Hall, 1988)

If you ask Doug, he'll say that LEAP is one of the best things we did during those critical turnaround years. I designed the program based on my research of common characteristics of a leadership program, but Doug is the one who had the guts to roll it out, allowing us to improve our performance as an organization.

In the "The Growth Years" section of the book we will provide an overview of START, our other significant leadership development program.

For individuals already in senior management roles, or being considered for them, we conduct individual assessments and from them create development activities tailored to their needs. Again, Bob Petrello, the "shrink on call," has been instrumental in conducting these assessments and coaching the individuals involved. The key factor is that we have made a commitment to ensure the success of our people by developing them prior to their taking on a new leadership role.

We take succession planning very seriously at Sundt and have done so for quite a while. We believe it is a primary responsibility of the current senior leadership of the company to provide for the systematic and orderly transition of leadership.

Not long after Gold Canyon we started formal succession planning. The top leaders of the company were asked to identify up to three successor candidates, provide an assessment of when they would be ready, and identify the specific developmental activities each successor would focus on during the year.

While we have been at this for a while, we frankly still have a way to go in ensuring that we have someone ready for each key role in the company. While filling leadership roles from within is our preference, we have not been able to do so in all cases because we just did not have the right person on board at the right time, or they were not developmentally ready for the assignment. It is good to bring some new blood in from the outside occasionally as it stimulates new thinking for those caught up in the Sundt paradigm.

Particularly due to the ongoing efforts of Dave Crawford, we have all made succession planning a priority, and for good reason. The very sustainability of the organization is dependent upon ensuring that constant attention is paid to the development of the succeeding generations of leaders for the company.

Building Blocks

1) The company had paid very little attention to succession planning, illustrated by Doug's experience when he was named President. At the division level, length of service was the primary criterion for replacing managers and very little had been done to prepare these individuals for their new role. Just prior to Gold Canyon, the company began to seriously address succession planning.

   a) Does your company have a system for succession planning?

   b) How far down the organization chart does your succession planning go? Only the top one or two levels, or down to other key managers?

   c) Once potential successors are identified, are there strategies and plans to help prepare those individuals for their potential future roles?

2) The company used an outside leadership development program (Center for Creative Leadership) to help the existing senior management team address immediate issues. One of the outcomes of that experience was the realization that future managers needed to have that type of training much earlier in their careers.

    a) Would your current senior leadership team benefit from an intensive outside leadership development program?

    b) Would an assessment of current leadership styles and skills help current leaders become more effective?

    c) Would an outside leadership experience serve as a catalyst to encourage other leadership development programs or experiences in your organization?

3) One of the most significant efforts in the transformation was clearly the creation of the LEAP program for the managers identified through the succession planning process. Nearly 50 percent of the senior management of the company has now completed that program, which is now in its fourth iteration.

    a) Does your company have a leadership development program?

    b) Is your program designed to address the specific leadership skills needed in your organization, and to promote and support collaboration among future leaders?

    c) Does your program effectively leverage both internal and external resources to provide a quality experience?

Chapter 8

INVESTING IN TECHNOLOGY

In order to grow and prosper, a company must be willing to invest in good technology that drives productivity and quality. At Sundt we've invested a lot into our IT equipment, our estimating and scheduling programs, our project administration systems, and our building information modeling (BIM), which allows us to develop 3D models of project plans identify and resolve construction issues during the design phase so they don't become costly problems later. We have also developed the remote office construction kit (ROCK), a handheld unit in the field with software that allows an employee and subcontractor to access every document they need on the job. Technology enhancements are not limited just to computers. It also applies to the concrete forming systems, concrete placing and finishing equipment, and other devices that help us drive productivity and improve quality.

The bottom line is that you must be willing to invest. Instead of asking whether you can afford to invest, ask if your company can afford not to. Remember that you should always expect a return on your investment, including technology. If this is not the case, your investment immediately falls into the category of bad technology. These are the fads, trends, and poorly researched impulse purchases that your people may be *really* excited about, but do nothing to improve quality and productivity. There is also a fear factor involved, which leads people to believe that if they don't take this action immediately, they might fail.

Resist employees' pleas of "We need to do this now!" and look into what you're investing in before pulling the trigger. Take the time to understand it, drill down to the detail of costs and return on investment, and make sure it will increase productivity and quality. If it doesn't do any of those things, don't spend money on it.

For instance, there are many accounting software systems out there, and most of them require and costly software upgrades. At one point we were thinking about designing our own. We spent a lot of money and realized a year later that we were nowhere close to where we thought we'd be. In hindsight we see that even if we had finished the process and rolled out our own Sundt accounting and project management software, we never would have been able to keep up with the demands of such a complex system. We were unknowingly digging a hole to jump into that could have been avoided by having a healthy discussion about the pros and cons of the idea. Remember that whenever you write a big check for new technology, it's going to be expensive both in terms of money and the time people spend away from their core jobs implementing it. Weigh all the information and options and make sure it's worth it.

During our crisis years, all of our company information was housed in a centralized data processing center. A reflection of Sundt's long-time closed-book mentality, none of the information was shared and most employees didn't know how to get to it.

After Gold Canyon, when we became a much more open-book and transparent company, we also opened access to most of the previously locked-up data. We started investing in technology, bringing modern computer equipment to the desks of all our people and Sundt into the twenty-first century. We also started investing in technology that would drive productivity, improving quality, significantly upgrading our estimating, project scheduling, contract management, and customer-contact management capabilities. In many ways our technology just a couple of decades ago was more like a boat anchor. Today it's a tool that truly enhances our performance as a company.

One of the things we learned from Jim Collins's books was this notion of technology as an accelerator. Technology is not the end but rather a means to an end. You can spend a lot of money on technology and really not improve efficiency or better manage knowledge. A number of really good companies spent a lot of money learning this lesson.

Building Blocks

1) In the mid 1990s the company was far behind other industries in the adoption of new technologies. Sundt began making thoughtful and significant investments in technology that would make us more efficient and more cost effective. In the construction industry, computerized modeling and digital records are just two of the trends where we have been early adopters. Technology is not just limited to computers but includes such items as concrete forming systems that make us more productive and improve quality.

    a) Is your company investing enough and investing in the right technologies to improve efficiency?

    b) Are you aware of and following industry innovations to remain competitive?

    c) Are you training your employees to use the new technologies to their maximum advantage?

2) Technology can help an organization become more productive, but not without a cost. You have to be willing to invest in technology and at the same time resist the temptation to chase every new trend. Technology investments, like any other investment, must have a return

on investment that makes business sense.

a)   Does your company investigate the ROI of technology purchases?

b)   Do you avoid developing customized applications that are costly to create and difficult to maintain?

c)   Do employees and managers understand your company's philosophy and process regarding the investigation and adoption of new technologies?

Chapter 9

ASSET MANAGEMENT

When you're losing money and trying to figure out what to do about it, you inevitably start looking at everything under the company umbrella. Equipment, land, each subsidiary company, each division—everything you own is an asset and whether you've reached the edge of a financial abyss or not, you need to ask yourself: Are these assets doing what you originally intended them to do? Are they earning money or making you more productive? If fixing something about the asset will solve the problem, then fine, fix it and move on. But if your assets are not earning money and don't fit into your plan, you must give serious thought to selling or closing them.

In 1998 many Sundt assets, from our equipment fleet to unused land, were not making money and needed to be fixed, sold, or closed to ensure our survival in the present and contribute to our growth in the future. However, just like any other project, we needed a plan before we took action. We needed to figure out what we were ultimately working toward and what steps we needed to take to get there.

All of our decisions to fix, sell, or close were based on our rolling ten-year plan. We closed a couple businesses that were ailing, such as Sundt Products and an internet/data/telecommunications business we had acquired that simply did not fit into our ten-year plan.

Our international division, in particular, needed to have some attention paid to it. We had been reasonably successful with international work in the past, but we needed to focus our efforts on being successful here at home for the foreseeable future, so we made the decision to shut down the entire operation. We also closed our industrial division because it lacked employees with the skill sets necessary to ensure the division survived and was profitable, and we didn't have the resources available to address that problem.

We were getting pressure from all directions to shut down our highway division. We had a lot of money tied up in its heavy equipment, and the division was performing very poorly. But based on our ten-year plan, the better decision was to figure out how to fix the problems and turn the division into a profitable one. The bottom line was that the success of the highway division was an integral piece of the 1-100-10 BHAG and it therefore needed fixing, not closing. This became a battle and a test of leadership.

We started by terminating much of the group's management because they had been responsible for taking on a lot of risky projects and losing money on most of them.

In Doug's words:

We hired a new manager and made some more adjustments within the division, but even with these changes, very little progress was being made. The bigger the changes we needed to make to ensure the highway group's survival, the greater the stubbornness and resistance we encountered.

Why did I have such a difficult time implementing the big changes that needed to be made to fit the highway group into our 1-100-10 plan? I was a 'building guy' and they were highway guys so there was a lack of trust. I was told, several times, "You don't understand; you don't come from our world." They weren't going to go along with any of my ideas, even if the ideas made sense, simply because they didn't trust me.

There was one guy I thought the highway group would trust and listen to. His name was Tedd Jones, and he was the predecessor of the manager we had to let go. When Tedd was running the highway division, Sundt was one of the most formidable contractors in the West. I had worked with Tedd for many years and had tremendous respect for his skill and leadership abilities. So we called Tedd to see if he would be interested in coming out of retirement and helping us fix this division. He also had to help us convince them they needed to make a lot of changes that would run counter to their current thinking, but needed to be made if they were going to survive as a division.

After I first called him and we were having coffee, Tedd looked at the five years of struggling highway-group financials and asked me point blank why I didn't close down the whole group. I told him, "Because as a young man I watched you work your magic, and you were the best." We needed someone to put this division back together and I knew I couldn't do it. If Tedd turned me down; I would have closed the group immediately.

Fortunately Tedd loved Sundt and always enjoyed a challenge, so he said yes, promising to give us twenty hours a week, but as it turned out he consistently gave us much more. He jumped in, teaching, training, developing, and most importantly communicating to the division what needed to be done and why. We were able to use Tedd to get the employees to do things that needed to be done because they believed in him and trusted him. He was able to develop them into a very productive and successful part of Sundt that has made major contributions ever since.

"Tedd is eight-two years old," Doug explains, "and still has an office here that he visits from time to time. He will always have an office here because we owe him such a debt of gratitude."

Our federal division faced similar challenges. It had been performing very poorly and was not in a good position to compete for work in the future that would help us meet our 1-100-10 plan. So, we hired a new manager, shuffled folks around, and made some decisions that would hopefully position the organization to get back on its feet. Unfortunately the new manager and his team inherited some significant projects that were losing lots of money. I knew it would take them time to work through these problems, but some other people weren't convinced they could do it.

Part of my role was to fend off a lot of questions from board members, sureties and others on why this division wasn't being closed. It's difficult to say you have faith in this new team when the financial numbers didn't suggest that. They didn't create these problems; they were just trying to manage through them while getting new work and growing their division.

As a new team, they did a very good job of navigating through all of these problems, bringing on new talent and obtaining new work. Today the federal division is a major contributor to this company and deserves a lot of credit. Federal agencies, particularly the Department of Defense, are among our most significant customers.

We owned a lot of underutilized equipment.

Shortly after I was named President of Sundt, I remember looking out the window of the Tucson facility at the vast expanse of equipment and land. To the untrained, civilian eye this may have looked impressive: rows and rows of equipment, nicely lined up on acres of land. But when you're footing the bill and none of it is being used, it's not a good sign. I knew what needed to be done, and I knew that people wouldn't like it.

We continued to dig, looking for things to fix, close, or sell that would bring in money and move us away from the edge of the abyss. The answers were coming fast and furious. Sundt seemed to be drowning in divisions that hadn't been profitable in years. We had land that was just sitting there, and cash-draining assets that we continued to own. Why was this? Part of the answer was a construction industry paradigm that said owning is better than leasing.

However, logic would tell you that if you own an asset and it's not making money, there's no point in keeping it around. We had rows of bulldozers, scrapers, backhoes, and other heavy construction equipment, which, for the most part, was highly underutilized. That equipment sat on twelve acres of land and required a five-bay maintenance facility to keep it running. Our industry has the tendency to own maintenance shops, proud of the fact that we can tear a piece of equipment to the ground and put it back together. The paradigm is that an equipment fleet saves money because you can own it cheaper than you can rent it. In our case this certainly wasn't true. The acres of land to park the underutilized equipment on, the maintenance facility, paying the mechanics, and so on, was causing us to lose millions of dollars each year.

The decision we made sent big waves of resistance throughout the company: we would sell 60 percent of that equipment; we would only own what we regularly used, turning it over on a scheduled basis, and rent what we used periodically, and—counter to the rest of the industry—own no maintenance facility. Our equipment fleet now contributes significantly to our bottom line. In addition, selling most of our equipment fleet and closing the maintenance shop allowed us to sell the building and the land it sat on. The asset sales didn't stop there. In Arizona we had two warehouses within one hundred miles of each other, supplying our jobs with small tools and equipment. We shut down one of the warehouses and sold most of its inventory. By doing this we freed up a lot of funds and made more money by leasing the empty warehouse and some yard space to a third party. We also sold five acres of adjacent land we weren't using. The proceeds from these sales were invested in more training and development and in technology that would drive productivity and quality.

We also owned 428 acres of land northwest of downtown Albuquerque where the company for many years had operated a sand and gravel plant. After the business was sold in the 1980s, Sundt continued to receive royalties from the new owner for the materials they mined. In 1998 the resources were pretty well exhausted, and we needed to decide whether to sell the raw land (a big hole in the ground) or reclaim it and develop it.

Our outside advisory board at the time was very vocal about selling this land to bring in cash, essentially saying that we had no business playing the role of a developer. That was probably very good advice that I should have listened to but didn't. I had watched Sundt sell some very valuable assets to fill in the holes created by construction losses. Assets can be like ATM machines. I was bound and determined that we would not sell this land or other assets to fill in another hole. I was sending a message that we were going to make a profit in our core businesses, and when we sold an asset, it was to put icing on the cake."

Led by Ray Bargull, our CFO, we had our Heavy Civil Division reclaim the land and put in the infrastructure needed for a large, modern subdivision. Then we sold off the land in parcels to local developers. This was a very successful project for the Albuquerque community, and it was financially very successful for the shareholders of Sundt.

It may seem drastic to some, having to fix, close, or sell such a large number of assets in such a short period of time. How did it get to this point? We had been a very project-centered company. A lot of our decisions were based on winning bids and competing to get projects: "If we do X, Y, Z, we will get the job." What we had to do was change our mindset and become a business-centered company. Yes, it is true that we are also an accumulation of projects, but it's still a business overall. We should have a certain expectation of what an asset should produce for us. And if it does not, it must be fixed, closed, or sold. No exceptions.

Building Blocks

1) In 1998 it was clear that the company had to address a series of problems with underperforming divisions. Doug's philosophy became "fix it, sell it, or close it," and that criterion was applied to each of those groups. We sold a couple, closed a couple, and worked on fixing the others. Our highway and federal divisions were two that we felt had the potential to be successful and we worked hard to fix.

   a) Do you have parts of your business that are not contributing?

   b) Have you asked yourself the question, "Should we sell it, close it, or fix it?"

   c) Do you have the courage and resources to do that?

2) Construction companies, historically, like to own a lot of equipment. Much of the equipment we owned was not being used and was not producing revenue. In the face of considerable opposition, Doug had a significant portion of our equipment fleet sold, and our internal maintenance facility closed. Today, our smaller, more productive fleet

is a source of significant revenue and margin.

a) Do you have nonproductive assets that you are holding onto because of tradition?

b) Do you have good accounting systems to show the contribution to revenue and margin for the assets you own?

c) Do you need to sell or replace older equipment and/or outsource equipment rental and maintenance?

Chapter 10

THE VALUE OF SERVICE

One very important aspect of turning a company around is- maintaining the values that have been such an important aspect of this company since its founding. We needed to generate some pride about our business and what business is about. We wanted people to be proud of the fact that this was a company that was making a difference.

This also gave us the opportunity to focus on what James Collins referred to in his book *Good to Great* as level-five leadership. We wanted our employee owners to learn the value of putting the company and others first. We believed if they would do this, that they would actually be more successful and so would Sundt. This is something that more businesses in America should either teach or model.

When it came time to redevelop our mission and vision statement for Sundt, words like *biggest* or *best* were very much part of the discussion. But when you slap the blinders on and only think about making money, you will never focus on the components of a good business. We felt it was important for our mission to be about service, community activism, and making a difference. Of course you have to make money in order to invest in your business and give back to the industry and community, but simply making lots of money should never be a business's primary focus. As it turns out, the more money we have given to charities in recent years, the more active our employees have been in improving their communities, the more successful Sundt has been as a business. We have seen a direct correlation between our investment in the nonprofit arena and company profits. To be clear, this is a blessing and a byproduct, not what motivated us to take a critical step in this area and establish our own charitable foundation.

The foundation began operations in 1999 as a direct result of our desire to provide employees with a vehicle for directly improving the lives of the less fortunate in their communities. In Doug's words: "This is something I wanted to do because I felt that giving back is something people should be doing. I'm very pleased with how it has worked and consider it my greatest success as CEO of Sundt."

We believe that a company has the responsibility to give back to its industry and the community. However, it would be wrong for us to take credit for what the Sundt Foundation has accomplished. We merely built upon an incredible existing foundation of giving. The Sundts as a family and as a company were active supporters of the community, local universities, and various charities over the years. While their support was solid and unwavering, it seemed for awhile that the charitable giving was coming almost entirely from the company and the employees were not individually involved.

The Sundt Foundation has changed that. Today more than seven hundred Sundt employees are members, and most support the foundation with weekly contributions from their paychecks. Sundt matches their contributions dollar for dollar, and also pays all of the administrative expenses (audits, etc.)   so every dollar an employee gives ends up being two dollars that go into improving the lives of the less fortunate. In 2011 the Sundt Foundation was approaching the $5 million mark in charitable giving.

Each of our offices has its own contributions committee, which reviews grant requests. The employees in those offices, not the executives at corporate, are the ones who basically decide which charities get grants, which range from $1,000 to $10,000. Our charitable efforts are directed toward improving the lives of disadvantaged children and adults. Over the years the ratio has been approximately 70 percent for children's issues and 30 percent for adult programs.

If that was where it stopped, the foundation would look like many other company-sponsored giving programs, but it doesn't. Our employees also volunteer their time in many different ways, such as participating in volunteer efforts, like fundraising walks, and cooking or serving at soup kitchens. As a company of builders, we have skills that most people don't have, so our employee-volunteers often step in to help charities like Habitat for Humanity build much-needed care facilities and homes for disadvantaged families. We enjoy building with our hands because that's what we do every day.

The Foundation's largest volunteer effort is the Mike Gaines Charitable Fundraising Events. Mike Gaines was a member of the Sundt family for almost twenty years. He worked on projects in the United States and around the world. His last foreign assignment was in 1997 as a senior project manager at the U.S. Embassy in Moscow. While in Moscow, Mike started experiencing the first symptoms of Amyotrophic Lateral Sclerosis (ALS), known as Lou Gehrig's disease. He was diagnosed in 1999 and shortly thereafter was forced into retirement. Mike knew there was nothing that could be done for him, but he wanted to be able to help others in the future. It was his idea to have a golf tournament to raise money for the Muscular Dystrophy Association's research efforts to find a cure for ALS.

The first golf tournament was held in Tucson in May 2001, and Mike was still well enough to attend. After his death the following year, the Tucson tournament became an annual event. Today tournaments are also held in Phoenix, San Diego, Sacramento, and San Antonio. There's also a Fun Skeet Shoot (another of Mike's favorite pastimes) in Tucson every fall. In 2012 we expect the event to surpass the one million dollar mark in funds raised for ALS research.

To learn more about the Foundation's work please visit http://www. sundtfoundation.org and we have both personally pledged all of this book's ongoing royalties to further its efforts. In Doug's words: Sundt Foundation is something I hope future leaders don't disband. The foundation means that Sundt is a company making a difference in people's lives. I hope it becomes a permanent part of our DNA. It means we are much more than just about building things; we are a company with a big heart.

Building Blocks

1) Although Sundt had a long tradition of community involvement, most of the company's financial contributions to charitable foundations came only from the company. Employees were not involved in either contributing to or selecting the recipients. Doug established the Sundt Foundation in 1999 and the foundation matched employee contributions dollar for dollar. To date, the Sundt Foundation has exceeded $5 million in contributions to worthwhile organizations in the communities where we live and work.

    a) Do you believe that a company has an obligation to give back to the communities where you live and work?

    b) Would your employees welcome the opportunity to become involved in supporting worthwhile charitable organizations?

    c) Do you have a vehicle for providing this opportunity for your company and your employees?

2) Beyond financial support, community service can include volunteer efforts. Many of the employees in our company have valuable construction skills that can be leveraged to help local organization. Over the years Sundt employees have helped construct numerous facilities for local organizations that serve disadvantaged families and children.

    a) Do your employees have skills that can be leveraged to support worthwhile local organizations?

    b) Do your employees have an interest in getting involved in their communities?

    c) Can you help facilitate that involvement?

Chapter 11

EMPLOYEE OWNERSHIP

You may recall that in the history chapter we mentioned that, following the untimely death of John Sundt, a profit sharing plan was put in place and in 1972 that plan was replaced by a stock bonus trust that contributed shares of company stock to each eligible employee, ultimately creating a company owned by its employees. That was the beginning of the current employee stock ownership plan (ESOP) that defines the ownership structure of our company today.

In Richard's words:

When I came to Sundt in 1993 from the education field, I was amazed with the apparent, at best, lack of interest by the employees of Sundt with the ESOP, and many who were openly negative about the program. Here was a plan that put away, on my behalf, a percentage of my wages for my retirement with no contribution from me. Maybe it was because of my experience in the education world, but I just couldn't understand how anyone would not think that was a good deal. I, like most Americans, would not have had the discipline to save that money for my retirement.

In any case, during the years that followed establishment of the ESOP, it gradually became an entitlement program rather than an incentive to perform at a higher level. This was largely due to the erratic performance of the company. People had just not seen the relationship between performance and increasing their personal wealth, which of course is the real power of employee ownership. At the time, federal law would have made it difficult for Sundt to have a 401k, which was the most common form of retirement benefit offered by construction companies. In most cases the contributions Sundt was making to employees' ESOP accounts exceeded what other employers were matching in their employees' 401k accounts. In all fairness, during some of this time the equity markets were making big gains and people felt they were missing out on that chance to grow retirement wealth that might have occurred if they were in a 401k program. As we all know, that big run-up in the '90s was followed by a major sell-off, which in many cases wiped out the gains that had been achieved earlier.

The way an ESOP is intended to work is very simple: the ESOP does well when you run your business well. Individual shareholder value is a direct reflection of how the company is performing. When employees have ownership in the company, they have the direct opportunity to impact their own wealth creation. This concept makes their role much different than being just an employee earning a wage. When an employee owner adds value to the company with a new idea, it adds value for the entire organization. Everyone benefits or is negatively affected by the actions of the individual owners of the company. This is the real power of employee ownership: the direct relationship between the employee's efforts and the performance of the company. The bottom line is that the more successful the company is, the more wealth is generated for the employee owners of the company.

However, the power of the ESOP had been anything but a good thing at Sundt. Even long-term employees had very small account balances after many years of service, the result of a long period of collective poor performance. That was about to change.

As we started to make the changes talked about in this section, our performance began to improve, and as it did, the employee owner's account balances started to grow. In fact, in just the last five years we have collectively created more wealth for the employee owners of Sundt than in all of the previous years of our history! Don't forget, as we write this book, we are 121 years old.

Today we know the power of employee ownership. We have witnessed the direct relationship between our actions and creation of retirement wealth. In his book *Good to Great* Jim Collins talks about the "flywheel concept." Picture a flywheel. If you give it a little push, it moves a little, and if you push it again, it rotates a little further. Keep pushing and you finally achieve a full rotation, which continues to pick up speed as long as those pushes continue. Prior to 2002 no Sundt employee had over $1 million in their ESOP trust. Since 2002, 104 Sundt employees have opened their annual ESOP statements and been stunned to see an account balance in excess of $1 million. Some employees are still here, but many have retired with a degree of financial comfort they never dreamed of. The pushes we made at Sundt during the turnaround resulted in an ever better performing company, which in turn created larger and larger amounts of shareholder wealth.

Building Blocks

1) The untimely death of John Sundt was actually part of the impetus for employee ownership at Sundt. The original profit sharing plan transitioned over time to an employee stock ownership plan (ESOP) that today owns 100 percent of the company. The company makes an annual contribution to the employee's ESOP account, based on a percentage of that employee's wages.

   a) Is your company employee owned to any extent?

   b) If your company is privately held, would there be value in implementing an employee ownership program to provide for the long-term succession of the organization?

2) Employee ownership provides a direct connection between company performance and personal wealth. At Sundt our exceptional performance has helped many employees have the resources for a very comfortable retirement.

    a) If your company is employee owned, do employees see the connection between their performance, company success, and their own financial future?

    b) If your company is not employee owned, are there other opportunities for employees to see direct benefit from their efforts and their financial success?

    c) Do employees have access to information about the company's financial performance?

SECTION III

THE GROWTH YEARS, 2005–2011

ACCELERATING THE TURNAROUND

Chapter 12

GROWING THE BUSINESS

By the end of 2004 we had made a lot of progress as a company. We had repaired our balance sheet, paid off all our debt, built up decent cash balance, and increased our investment accounts. The performance of our operating units had improved dramatically, and as a company, we were now consistently meeting or exceeding our goals.

We had become more disciplined and more focused. Our strategic planning process was working extremely well, helping us become more strategic in our thinking and much less reactionary to current events. Our investments in training and development, technology, and succession planning were really paying off. We had elevated a lot of people to new positions, and they were ready to successfully take on new responsibilities.

Life had changed a lot around Sundt except that with all the time spent on repairing the ship we had not focused enough on growth.

In Doug's words:

It was now time to take that step as well. One of the most important things in moving forward and growing our business was to not lose sight of what got us here. We needed to maintain our discipline as we moved forward. One of the keys for getting this done and concentrating on growth was for me to split the roles that I had held as both CEO and COO.

I had come to the conclusion as to who the best choice for COO, was and I was comfortable with that decision. It was time for me to step up to chairman and CEO and promote Dave Crawford to president and COO.

Dave had been with Sundt since college. He is a civil engineer and has held several positions on the operating side of our building division. At the time of his promotion, Dave was senior vice president and manager of the building division. He had done an excellent job of improving the performance of our Arizona operations, which had always been one of our most consistent and profitable divisions. He was also spending a lot of time bringing more order to our California offices, both of which had struggled greatly and needed his leadership.

Splitting these positions let me spend more time on our strategic direction and succession planning. It also gave the opportunity to address governance issues and the improvement of our board of directors and its functions. I could also devote time to consulting with the managers of the service side of our business to see how we could continue to get better in these areas and how we could increase our other income by taking on and managing more risk that might enhance and support our operations. Finally, this change would give me more time to focus on investments that might improve our bottom line, not just now, but well into the future.

Since 2005 we have added three new outside board members, Ray Holdsworth, retired vice chairman of AECOM; Ron Ludwig, retired ESOP attorney; and Frank Brady, retired CPA at Ernst and Young, to diversify governance and to bring expertise and outside thinking that we didn't have. They are not only active participants at the board level, but they are also active participants on our Ethics Committee, ESOP/401k Committee and Audit Committee. They have brought a lot of experience and wisdom to the board and have been very insightful, helping us manage our business better.

We have purchased several acres of distressed properties, including a prime piece of property adjacent to Arizona State University, which should yield some nice returns for the shareholders of Sundt when we sell them in future years.

We have taken on additional risk with various insurance programs but have managed them extremely well. Because of the additional risk, our employees understand they must get better at safety, quality, subcontractor selection, and other activities, which has also helped improve our construction operations.

Since we paid down our debt and started to build up our cash reserves, we now manage our cash with an investment committee and investment managers. This was not an issue at Sundt in the past, but today it creates significant income for our company.

Splitting these roles also allows Dave to focus on continually improving our discipline as an organization, increasing our productivity and the quality of our performance. Dave now spends more time examining how we can begin to successfully grow the revenues and corresponding profits in each unit.

In 2004 our revenue was $583 million. We reached a high water mark in 2008 with revenues of $1.154 billion, just before the downturn in what turned out to be the greatest recession since the depression of the 1930s. This essentially doubled our revenues in four years. We also had record profits in 2008 despite the fact that the economy was in a dramatic downturn.

Throughout the company we continue to push discipline and continually make improvements in our training and development programs and in our use of technology. We have continued to expand our capabilities in building information modeling (BIM), as well as in the use of programs that improve efficiency at the project level and create virtual buildings on a computer right before the client's eyes to establish cost models before design has even begun.

We are also a company that takes great pride in building certain parts of a project ourselves, rather than subcontracting that work. As someone who has hired skilled workers to perform concrete, site development, utilities, process piping, and equipment setting, Dave knows what it takes to improve productivity and quality.

Dave has also invested time in looking at our business development efforts so we can ramp up the growth and gain some consistency at getting work and adding to our list of customers. He has worked with Richard and some outside consultants to further improve this effort.

Since I announced over two years ago that Dave would be my replacement, Dave has also spent a lot of time taking courses in risk management, accounting and finance, ESOPs, and other subjects, increasing his knowledge in areas that he has not previously been exposed to.

As I stated earlier, in the first few years of the turnaround I was a rather autocratic leader, and for what I think were the right reasons at the time. It's not necessarily the best way to run a company, but at the time I didn't think I had any choice. Could we have split those duties sooner? Maybe, but there were a lot of extenuating circumstances that prevented me from making that decision; today I'm glad to see how it worked out.

I know Dave is thinking seriously about splitting the role of COO into two positions, helping to reduce their number of people who report directly to him and giving the co-COOs more time to work with their respective profit center managers, since we have a fairly aggressive growth plan for the next ten years. This will also provide ample time to focus not only on growth but on maintaining and improving what we have accomplished to date. A great team has been assembled to successfully guide this company to our next ten-year goal.

Building Blocks

1) In the life of a business, if you are not growing the organization, you begin reducing the return on equity and reducing the opportunities for your employees to advance and develop their careers. Once the more serious issues at Sundt were being addressed, we needed to start focusing on growth.

   a) Is your company growing?

   b) If not, do you understand the need to grow?

   c) Do you have strategic plans that will guide your company's growth?

2) In the early days of the transformation, Doug held the role of CEO and COO because he needed to retain a close relationship with the operating divisions. By 2004 it seemed to make sense to split those roles so that Doug could focus more attention to growing the company.

   a) Do you have the right organization structure and leadership to manage current operations and long-term growth?

   b) Have you developed leaders to support the growth of the organization?

3) During the late 1990s Doug established an advisory committee to get an external perspective on the issues facing the company. That concept was formalized with the addition of three outside members of the board of directors, and those individuals have helped the company make a more candid assessment of its current status and future needs.

   a) Does your organization structure provide for external governance?

   b) If not, do you solicit input from credible individuals outside your organization?

Chapter 13

BUSINESS DEVELOPMENT

In the first five years of the turnaround we focused on stopping the bleeding and the issues we talked about in Section II. As those changes started to take hold we could begin to focus on other issues like growing revenues.

Revenue growth had not been a priority since we were focused on growing profits, or what we refer to as margins. There is an old saying that margin thrills and revenue kills. What is the point of doing a billion dollars of work and making little or no profit? You might have some bragging rights for a year or two with your construction buddies, but with no profits there is little chance of sustaining the organization.

But as we started to perform with discipline and our profitability improved, it became apparent that we had to start growing the top line of the company at a rate that exceeded inflation and fixed costs like wage increases. By this time we were not content with just being average. We wanted to produce best-in-class returns for the employee owners of Sundt.

Sundt had celebrated operational excellence over the years and had not paid a lot of attention to business development and top-line growth. This was not uncommon in the industry, but as our customers became more sophisticated in making their buying decisions, business development started to be something we really needed to address, and the reason is really very simple: *If you don't have work, nothing else much matters!*

One of the early indications that business development was not a part of our culture at Sundt was that business development managers were paid significantly less than their counterparts in operations and preconstruction (estimating), although all had similar responsibilities. Again, this was not unique to Sundt, as the industry was for the most part structured this way. We didn't have job descriptions for the various roles in business development, and from profit center to profit center, positions in business development with the same title had very different responsibilities.

Finally, and very importantly, the path to senior management did not go through business development, but rather through operations or preconstruction. Doug, our chairman and CEO, had come up primarily through the estimating side, and Dave Crawford, our COO, rose through operations, and that was also true for the senior managers in the profit centers. Again, while this kind of culture was common in the construction industry, it is amazing when you think about it since most other industries reward sales positions with money and promotion opportunities.

One of the first things we did was make the business development managers' compensation equal to that of the operations and precon managers. With those changes came added expectations, and we initially lost, or had to let go, several people who had been in this role but just could not meet expectations or were uncomfortable with the expanded responsibilities. We established a set of organizationally consistent job descriptions for the various business development roles, and again, some folks moved on who did not have the required skills. All of these moves and others we made sent a clear message to the employee- owners of the company that doing "good" work was job one.

One of the next steps we took was to use a tactic that had worked well for us in several other areas, which was to find an outside consultant to evaluate our business development and marketing efforts. We developed a consultant agreement with David Pugh, one of the two founders of the Lore International Institute. Dave was a recognized thought leader in this area and had consulted with many companies, including construction companies. Dave saw in Sundt a willingness to take seriously his experience-based suggestions and improve our business development processes. We first had him present at one of our leadership academies. Dave is an accomplished and humorous speaker, and he hit it off quite well with most of the people present. Prior to the academy we had distributed copies of Dave's book *The Behavioral Advantage*, which uses the analogy of a chess game to illustrate his thoughts on how to effectively win work.

The key here is that we were smart enough to know that we needed an outside look at our practices, and Dave was smart enough to take the time to figure us out and work within our culture.

Dave's views were an instrumental part of improving our business development processes using the early, middle and end (chess) game model. Dave's key point, which reinforces the notion of simplicity on the far side of complexity, is that the most important differentiator in business development is when you stop selling and start helping your customer buy. Another way of saying the same thing is that success is as simple at being better than your competition in understanding what *they* want and offering up solutions to those needs—*being a customer-focused business.*

To be sure, in our business a certain amount of the work is won through low price. In those cases, while relationships are not unimportant, you still have to be the low cost provider. A low bid in most cases never creates the best value for the customer. Our job was to work harder at helping our customers understand the value of alternative ways of procuring construction services. In Arizona Dave Crawford was one the key individuals who worked to change the state procurement laws to allow for alternate procurement methods.

Sundt is becoming somewhat of an anomaly as a general contractor because of our market diversity and particularly our desire to perform certain aspects of the work ourselves, such as concrete, site, and utilities work. But that diversity has benefited us greatly in the recent deep recession that started in 2008. We also benefited from the early steps we took to improve our business development processes. Another important aspect of our improvement in business development is market analysis, or as we like to call it, "Where is the money?" Prior to the turnaround, we had gotten in a rut, working just in markets where we had experience, which of course is not a bad strategy for success. However, markets shift over time, sometimes very rapidly. You have to be constantly on top of the trends, and respond to them if you want to grow your business. Again, we looked externally for help with this issue. What we needed was a way to build upon our own market intelligence and the data we purchased each year from a national company that forecasts construction industry trends. We found the answer in Dr. Kim Nelson, who teaches services marketing at the University of Arizona. Not only is he extremely knowledgeable about market forecasting, but his father also owned a construction company for many years, so Kim has a basic familiarity with our industry. Kim took the national data and combined it with our market experience to create forecasts tailored to Sundt. They have been invaluable in helping us grow our current markets as well as expand into new geographic areas.

At this time we added a corporate marketing plan to our corporate strategic plan as a means of systematically identifying markets that would provide growth opportunities for the company. We started with eleven different geographical areas for possible domestic expansion, and through a very analytical process selected two of those areas for initial development. We expanded to the first market, Texas, in 2010 and expect to move into the next one within the next year or two. In the past, market expansion decisions were for the most part emotionally driven or completely opportunistic, but our process now starts analytically, and we then add our past experience and emotion to the decision. For us, this process has resulted in much better decisions regarding geographic and market expansion.

We continue to evaluate our business development effort to be sure we have the right people involved. Again, for most of our history, we were a company that celebrated operations and preconstruction services, and many of those people just did not celebrate the pursuit of work; it just was not their thing. So we have had to move some folks around, hire some new ones, and over time create a different culture of career development that recognizes the value of those who are good at selling work. In that regard, the last four senior management positions that we filled were all with people who had been directly involved in business development. So the message is clear: demonstrated skill in getting work is a career enhancer at Sundt.

As they say, the proof of the pudding is in the eating. By 2008 we had more than doubled our revenues while sustaining and even improving our profitability. While placing a focus on business development seems almost ridiculous in the rear view mirror, the point is that during this turnaround we made significant changes to our culture, and we did not just focus on the things that moved us away from the abyss. We worked on issues that positioned the company for a sustained and profitable future.

Building Blocks

1) The construction industry tends to focus on and honor operations (building), but in reality if you don't have a good system of business development, none of that matters. Like many companies, Sundt did not appear to value business development, but in an increasingly competitive marketplace that needed to change. The compensation for business development managers was elevated to be on a par with operations and estimating managers, and their expectations were raised to match that. Today, business development is much more a part of our culture at Sundt.

   a) Do you value business development?

   b) Is your organizational structure and compensation system evidence of the value you place on that function?

   c) Do you have the best possible people in your business development roles?

2) Construction clients in today's market want to talk to people who know how to build. Therefore, it is not practical to hires sales professionals from other industries; we need to develop sales skills in construction professionals. With the help of some great consulting and a lot of attention we have refined our sales tools and skills to become much

more effective in business development.

a) What types of individuals are most effective in your industry in the business development role?

b) Do you clearly understand the buying expectations of your prospective clients?

c) Do your business development personnel have the right tools and the right skills to be successful?

3) Sundt is somewhat unique in our industry because we are highly diversified. We are a commercial building contractor, highway contractor, industrial contractor, federal contractor and more. Gathering data about those various marketplaces takes considerable time and effort. But it is important to "follow the money." To improve our expertise in market research, we hired a university professor to help us understand the existing data and analyze it to support our business development needs.

a) Do you have access to good market research data?

b) Do you have internal or external expertise in analyzing and interpreting that data?

c) Do you have good internal processes for gathering and adding local and anecdotal data to the more formal data to get a true picture of business opportunities?

Chapter 14

THE ONLY CONSTANT IS CHANGE

> *"Success comes from your ability to manage change."*
>
> Doug Pruitt

It seems clear that successful organizations of all kinds going forward will have two closely related characteristics: they will be good at change and innovative. We define being good at change as minimizing the negative impact of the change and the speed at which the change can be executed.

When we look back at the turnaround years, everything was changing as we scrambled to get the company back on a solid footing. It is a general rule that any organization has a limited capacity for change and in hindsight it is amazing that we were able to institute the number of changes that we did during the turnaround, but then again we really did not have a choice. A very positive outcome of the turnaround is that we have developed a high capacity for change, and we learned that this would serve us well as we grew.

So as we started to focus on growth, even though we didn't realize it, we had in our kit of tools a group of individuals who had been able to manage a lot of change. But while we had developed the capacity, we would learn that we had a lot to learn about effectively managing the change process.

As we mentioned earlier in this book, strategic management is really a structured way of managing change. It is a way of identifying where you want to go, where you are today, and the changes (strategies) that need to be made to bridge that gap. Strategic planning and management was helping us with making changes on a number of issues, but in spite of that, we were having trouble making changes efficiently to the Sundt Way (the organizational consistent policies and procedures of the company) as well as other strategic and tactical changes.

As the turnaround took hold and we started to turn our attention to growth, the employee owners of the company were gaining confidence and looking to find other ways of continuing to improve the performance of the company. In addition, we were moving away from the low trust environment that had characterized the early years of the turnaround and individuals had greater operational flexibility to innovate. Those sound like good things and indeed they were, but because we did not have a systematic way of managing change at the time, there were some negative consequences.

The first problem was that we were learning that while we had implemented the Sundt Way, the organizationally consistent policies and procedures we expected to be followed by everyone in the company, the truth was that there was still a lot of inconsistency in the company about how these procedures were being executed. That problem existed largely because there was no systematic way for making changes to the Sundt Way. In addition, when changes were made, there was no way for all those entities that would be impacted by the change to weigh in on the change.

Next, we had some very creative individuals who took the initiative to identify a change that they thought would be helpful to the company. The problem was that people would incubate a change in a silo, and in the worst case scenarios we would find ourselves having to shut down a change initiative that an individual or several individuals had invested a lot of discretionary time in because it was not financially feasible, had not included in its development all those who would be impacted by it, and as a result did not anticipate some factors that would impact the usefulness of the change, or the change had been tried earlier and found not feasible.

Another problem was that we struggled with how to solicit and evaluate best practices and make them available to those who needed them. There had been several attempts to do this in previous years, but in some cases we had no way of easily categorizing those practices and making them available to those who needed them in the company. On the other hand, when we did get best practices identified and catalogued, we just did not see them being utilized.

Finally, we received feedback that for some of our folks we were simply making too many changes without providing sufficient communications on the purpose of the change and the training to support the change, and we were not giving the change time to be fully implemented and have its value evaluated.

So we had some folks, who had been observing these issues, come up with what they thought was a solution. Paul Levin in our Safety Department a creative personality. He was one of those who listened to our people in the field and observed that we did not have a systematic way of making changes to the Sundt Way, and he was also concerned about the poor implementation and frequency of change. Terri Babcock, our knowledge management specialist, had a front row view of the continued inconsistencies in the Sundt Way and the problems we were having in systematically making changes to it.

These individuals championed the need for a cross-functional committee of individuals who could manage changes to the Sundt Way. What resulted was *Kaizen* (Japanese for *improvement*), a name Paul suggested, which was adopted by the executive team. Kaizen would bring together the key perspectives that needed to be at the table when ideas for change to the Sundt Way and best practices were considered. Our IT Department helped provide a mechanism for anyone in the organization to submit an idea and they received immediate feedback electronically that their idea had been received. Those ideas would come to Terri, who would use her judgment to determine if the idea was something that would impact the Sundt Way or a best practice. All these ideas were placed in the Kaizen log that could be viewed by anyone in the company and the members of the Kaizen Committee.

At each monthly meeting of Kaizen, the team would review new items added to the Kaizen log and confirm or make changes in how the submitted idea would be categorized: Sundt Way or best practice. In some cases the discussion would lead immediately to the decision that the idea would not move forward. The submitter of the idea was notified electronically and in most cases personally by Terri, who expressed appreciation for idea and explained Kaizen's decision for not moving the idea forward in the process. If the idea moved forward, it would be assigned to the Kaizen team representative who was in the best position to vet it more fully. That person would recommend it to Kaizen if he or she believed it offered a needed change to the Sundt Way, or considered it a best practice that should be shared with the rest of the company.

We established an area on the company intranet called Sundt IQ where the best practices reside and are organized in a way that makes sense in our industry. Sundt Way changes are communicated monthly to the entire company and more quickly to those most impacted by the change.

Kaizen was taking us to the next level in managing change and initially had some very positive impacts. It provided an easy way for anyone in the company to submit an idea—your best ideas are usually bottom up, not top down, by the way.

Kaizen brought everyone to the table. So we started to see the benefits of collaborative decision making in which everyone had a chance to assess how the idea would impact their part of the business. It speeded up the change process in many cases but not always.

We had identified a way of making changes to the Sundt Way and we could identify best practices, which we had not had before.

But we still had some change management issues that were a problem, particularly as they related to items we came to call strategic and tactical initiatives. We also continued to have the problem of strategic and tactical initiatives not moving to a go/no go decision very quickly, primarily because the people who generated these ideas had "day jobs" and just did not have the time to move the initiative forward in a timely fashion. Finally, we continued to have the problem of someone's idea for change being thought out in a silo, and we had people spending time and effort on a change initiative for which they had a lot of passion that was not in some cases shared by others in the company.

Dave Crawford, our COO, made a presentation at our summer leadership academy on a more systematic set of steps that strategic and tactical initiatives should go through to help improve our success and efficiency in making change. At the same time, we had come across a book written by Juan Riboldi, who had researched the characteristics of how successful change is made. He developed the accent model, which illustrates the steps in executing a successful change. He believes you can make change using this model in a hundred days. We asked Juan to help us improve our ability to make change, and the first step was to transform our Kaizen process.

The Sundt version of the accent model is illustrated here:

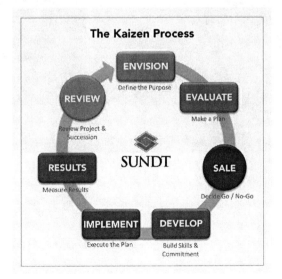

The Kaizen team was reconstituted as a Kaizen board of directors, and we now have a Kaizen executive director who champions the process full-time for a year at a time. The executive director takes a year's sabbatical to manage the Kaizen process. We hope that over time this will be seen as a career enhancer for the people who fill this role. Five kinds of initiatives are managed by Kaizen: strategic, tactical, Sundt Way, best practices, and continuous improvement. Strategic and tactical go/no go decisions are made by the executive management.

STEPS	DESCRIPTION
1 Envision	What is the desired outcome?
2 Evaluate	What is happening now? What actions are required to improve?
3 Sale	Should we do this?
4 Develop	How do we build skills and commitment?
5 Implement	Who is responsible for doing what?
6 Results	What results do we expect by when?
7 Review	Who should be involved in the future?

Building Blocks

1) As we became more competent at strategic management, we became increasingly aware that strategic management is really change management. In the early days we were trying to fix problems. But as we move forward, our strategic management process must adapt to finding new opportunities and changing the organization to succeed in a dynamic marketplace. We have to continually increase our capacity to change.

   a) Do you have a system for identifying the external influences on your business?

   b) Do you have a process for strategically changing the organization to meet those needs?

   c) Are you creating in your employees an increased capacity to change?

2) While the Sundt Way and our efforts for organizational consistency helped improve efficiencies, we needed to make sure we simultaneously encouraged innovation. Several "continuous improvement" programs had failed in the past, but in 2009 we implemented our Kaizen committee to focus on gathering, analyzing, and implementing employee suggestions for improvement. Although that is still a work in progress, we have refined the process and are beginning to see some significant improvements.

   a) Do you have process in place that encourages innovation?

   b) Do you have a process to carefully analyze both suggestions for improvement and critical business issues?

   c) Do you capture and make available the results of your continuous improvement efforts?

Chapter 15

CONTINUOUS IMPROVEMENT

Strategic Planning and Management

The strategic management process continued to mature as we moved to the growth years. The process added a corporate marketing plan that provided an analytical way based on third-party market data to validate our current markets and to identify potential new markets and geographies in which to grow the company. We took another step of improvement with the marketing plan by using a professor at the University of Arizona, Dr. Kim Nelson, to analyze the raw market data and provide an objective analysis of the information. This is another example of using an outside party to objectively provide expertise and to challenge our thinking.

As was mentioned earlier, the executive management of the company is responsible for the development of the corporate strategic plan, which is revisited every other year. Profit and service centers annually develop three-year rolling tactical plans that identify the specific tactics they will deploy to help the company meet its strategic goals. These tactical plans have become better aligned with the corporate strategic plan and more focused over the years to the point where they are really quite good and serve as the basis for how our profit and service centers are managed. The profit centers' tactical plans include what we call a mini-marketing plan for each of the markets the profit center is pursuing. These plans are developed by the champion(s) for that market, and they have become much better and indicate a deeper understanding of the market.

The executive management team is responsible to help ensure we reach our growth goal of tripling company revenues over the next ten years. Each of these growth strategies has been assigned champions in senior management to prepare a plan using the new Kaizen model illustrated earlier in the book.

Providing for the Orderly Succession and Development of Leadership

There are a couple of notable continuous improvements that the company initiated in the growth years. First, the LEAP program that was mentioned earlier had turned out to be a big success and we realized we needed something similar for people earlier in their careers at Sundt. The data are very clear that if you can keep someone in your company for approximately five years, it increases the chance of their staying with you longer. So we initiated Sundt Talent and

Recognition Training (START) for new employee owners—primarily engineers but also others from the support departments, estimating, and so on, who were in the first three years of employment. We planned a curriculum that gave them a broad view of their company, including strategic planning, operations, preconstruction, and business development. Bob Petrello worked with the participants on leadership development and team building activities and there were team projects. Just as we did with LEAP, Doug conducted the CEO forum, and they took several self-assessments that Bob provided feedback on. This program has also been successful, and we think it is helping our retention of talent in the early years while giving the participants a much broader view of their company than they might otherwise have.

Succession planning continues to be a central focus and we have developed some other processes to help senior managers understand the importance of developing successors for their roles. We also have been working to tie together the individual development plan process for performance assessment and career development to the succession planning process. We still have a way to go in this area to ensure this gets the attention it deserves so that we can provide for the orderly succession of competent leadership. We continue to be reminded of the advantage of having quality successors in place when you have an opening.

Technology

One of the important aspects of turning this company around was to get out of the dark ages as it related to technology. As painful as it was to spend money when we had a lot of debt and very little cash, we felt it was critical for us to invest in our future by purchasing technology that would help us drive productivity and improve quality.

We really wanted to become a leader in the deployment of technology rather that an also-ran. Today we are known as a company that is a leader in the construction industry in the productive use of technology, from programs that improve construction means and methods to building information modeling (BIM), LEAN construction techniques (to improve efficiency), ROCK (remote office construction kit,) D-profiler (a program for estimating the cost of a building before design begins), and many others.

As we take this company to the next level over our next ten-year strategic plan, it will be critical for us to take our use of technology to the next level as well. That will require us to stay abreast of what is going on in our industry and others so we can continue to make prudent investments in upgrading and adding technology that will help us drive productivity and improve quality.

We must also be very mindful of the fact that you can go broke chasing technology developments that yield very little, if any, benefit. We have to be smarter at separating the "I want" requests from the "I need" ones.

At Sundt, technology sets us apart. It will be important for future generations to make sure it stays that way.

Chapter 16

THE RESULTS

We started this book by sharing with you how a good company got into serious financial trouble and provided a fly on the wall look at the things we did to climb out of the hole we had made for ourselves. I suspect you wonder what the bottom line results were from the actions we collectively took to move away from the edge of the abyss. We think the following three charts illustrate the point that we not only filled in the hole but built a mountain of success.

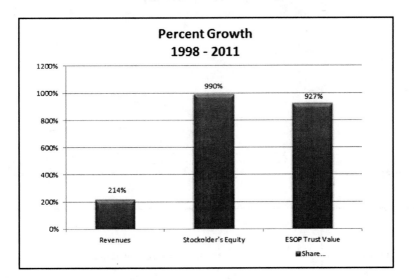

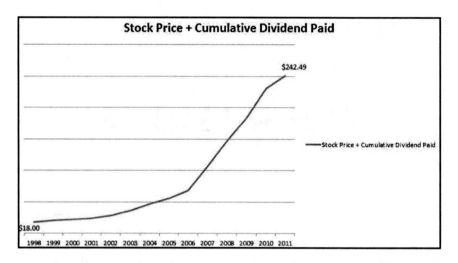

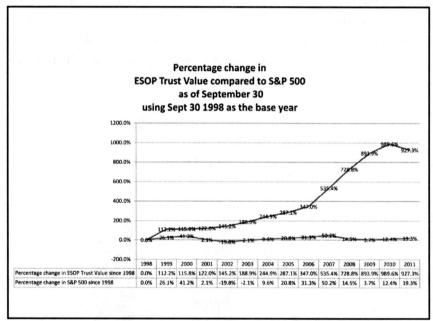

The proceeding charts illustrate the dramatic financial turnaround we have experienced at Sundt over the last eleven years. This change in fortune was accomplished without compromising our values. Our primary focus in this turnaround was to insure the sustainability of the company and just as importantly create value for the employee owners of Sundt. When we convened in Gold Canyon in 1996, our 106 year old company was silently on the verge of bankruptcy and with the exception of Wilson Sundt, no one had an ESOP stock balance of one million dollars or more. As these pages have revealed we not only survived the crisis, but the first employee millionaire in the ESOP occurred in 2002 and since that time, our collective efforts have produced 119 employee owners with ESOP balances of one million or more while exponentially outperforming the S&P 500.

SECTION IV

THE NEXT
120 YEARS

The Bridge Builder

by Will Allen Dromgoole

An old man, going a lone highway,
Came at the evening, cold and gray,
To a chasm, vast and deep and wide
Through which was flowing a sullen tide.

The old man crossed in the twilight dim;
The sullen stream had no fears for him;
But he turned when safe on the other side
And built a bridge to span the tide.

"Old Man," said a fellow pilgrim near,
"You are wasting strength with building here;
Your journey will end with the ending day;
You never again must pass this way;
You have crossed the chasm, deep and wide.
Why build you the bridge at the eventide?"

The builder lifted his old gray head.
"Good friend, in the path I have come," he said,
"There followeth after me today
A youth whose feet must pass this way.
This chasm that has been naught to me
To that fair-haired youth may a pitfall be.
He, too, must cross in the twilight dim;
Good friend, I am building the bridge for him."

Chapter 17

DON'T FORGET WHAT GOT US HERE

First we want to thank you for reading our book. We hope that there were a few nuggets of wisdom that you have learned from our experience that can help you with what you face in your company. We benefited greatly from the experiences of others in the turnaround of our company and if this book can be of that kind of help to others, it fulfills one of the two primary reasons we wanted to tell our story.

A recurring theme in this book is discipline, so as our story comes to an end we wanted to reinforce that theme one more time. When you lose your discipline, you should always expect to pay a penalty. It might not be today, tomorrow, or a year from now, but any period of lapsed discipline has consequences. Look at our nation's banks, for instance. They fell into poor lending practices in the 1980s, handing out money as if it were going out of style, and got hammered as a result. So they tightened their lending rules and restored order, but somewhere along the way lost their discipline again, and history repeated itself in 2008–2009.

This is a familiar story for many businesses, not just banking. They lose their discipline and often find it extremely difficult (or impossible in the cases of the ones that don't survive) to recover.

We got as close to the edge of the abyss as any business can, and for a while it looked like we might fall in, sending a good company with an incredible history plummeting to its death. We hope this book serves to tell that story, to warn other businesses that if it can happen to Sundt, it can happen to them. There are many books out there about turnarounds, but they are usually about major corporations. What we hope is that small and medium-sized businesses will realize that many of the things we have gone though, and many of the things we have done to correct our situation and return to a high level of profitability, can be done by any business, not just major corporations.

Most importantly we want this book to serve as a big, red caution sign to future generations of Sundt employees. We made a significant investment in our future by investing heavily in extensive training and development programs. We also invested heavily in technology accelerators that would drive productivity and quality. We studied our failings, learned from our mistakes, and started creating an organization that had the discipline to address its problems head-on. We institutionalized the processes to change many of the ways in which we had been conducting business and begin anew the process of moving this company forward. As stated in Jim Collins's book *Good to Great*, we were willing to face the brutal facts and do something about them. Because of the many changes we have instituted at Sundt, our employees will hopefully never have to experience these failings again as long as they maintain their discipline.

Some would say that we got lucky, and there is some truth to that. But if you rely on "luck" to get you through difficult times, you have eliminated all accountability for success or failure within your organization. We so often use "bad luck" as an excuse for bad behavior. Watch the news and listen to the talk of up cycles and down cycles of business and the economy. If you believe that your business is at the mercy of the world around you, what reason is there to be accountable for your actions? Conversely, imagine the news broadcast that announces, "There's no such thing as luck, only accountability. If your business is failing, it's your job to do something about it." How do you think that message would go over with what is increasingly becoming a woe-is-me public, always looking for a big corporation or politician to blame for all its problems?

We believe you make your own luck. Sure, there is a little luck involved in some things. In golf you can hit a bad shot that bounces off a tree and goes in the hole for a hole in one, but that kind of luck doesn't make you a good golfer, and surely doesn't get you where you want to be. What gets you there is discipline.

You can call it luck or brilliance, or some combination of both, but we made a lot of changes during the turnaround years that pulled us out of a nosedive and started us on our way to success. Neither luck nor brilliance will magically keep the same events from repeating themselves if you don't have the right processes in place and discipline ingrained in your company.

The lesson we learned is that the notion of discipline needs to be constantly reinforced in the organization. It seems to be a natural part of human behavior that, for a variety of reasons—things going on at home, too much work to do, the pressure to get work—people lose their discipline and the system breaks down.

Sundt will always have new leaders stepping up to take the helm in different profit centers or at the corporate level, and the more a company grows, the more dramatic the wake up calls can be. As time passes, and people travel farther and farther from the events that caused this story, it becomes institutional history and people will forget about the events that got us into so much trouble. The question we want future Sundt employees to always be asking themselves is: Have we created processes and discipline to prevent this from happening again? Are these lessons built deep into the DNA of Sundt?

People don't want to hear about 1996–1998 again. It's a new millennium now. They don't care. We know we can't talk about the turnaround story in terms of those years, but rather in terms of how we want to run the organization. We have worked hard to show our people what could happen in terms of loss of productivity and quality, financial risk, and other bad things that happen when you don't have process and discipline in place, and you aren't investing heavily in training and development and technology accelerators. If these lessons are built into the DNA of your company, they are no longer abstract concepts extracted from history; they are concrete.

You build the organization so these missteps cannot take on a life of their own and destroy you. You do it to lessen your chances of slipping. If you can implement the right things in your business, as Jim Collins states in his book, *Good to Great*, the flywheel starts spinning and takes on a life of its own. Everyone is keenly aware and paying attention now. This is how you want to run your business every day, every year, not because you're trying to dig yourself out of a deep hole, but because you want to sustain the progress that you have made and continue to advance your organization. The chances of drifting back to the edge of the abyss become less and less.

We came close to going out of business and now our performance has risen to the level that it should have been at and to the level of several of the competitors we admire and have great respect for. It's a great turnaround story, but the job is never really done. Change is inevitable, and you have to avoid thinking you have finally arrived.

Chapter 18

A MESSAGE TO FUTURE GENERATIONS AT SUNDT

One of the primary goals for this book is to pass on the lessons learned from this turnaround to the future leadership of Sundt. You don't get to the edge of the abyss and then execute a successful turnaround without learning a few things. Here are a few lessons in summary that we learned and while our primary audience is future generations of leaders at Sundt, we think these lessons may be equally applicable to your organization.

Lesson: First there were the lessons that came from decades of arrogance. With arrogance comes the tendency to don the blinders and slip into complacency, shedding discipline in favor of the thrill of perpetual motion. When you are in a dynamic business like ours, continuously hiring people without providing them the proper training, combined with a laidback attitude toward discipline, is a prescription for trouble.

Lesson: The trouble that we found ourselves in taught us that, as successful as we might be, we can never relax. We must always look at changes that need to be made, or we will fall back into trouble again. As soon as you think you are good enough and lose discipline, you're heading right toward the abyss again.

Lesson: One critically important lesson is that you are constantly bringing new people into the organization and they bring with them their previous experiences, which may or may not align with the expectations of your organization. In the midst of the turnaround we made a renewed effort to attract new talent to the organization. That was a good thing for us. However, we did not initially do a good a job of on-boarding these new people and getting them up to speed on the Sundt Way, our disciplined approach to the organizationally consistent company procedures and policies. The result was that some of these folks simply practiced what they had been taught or what they had previously experienced, which was inconsistent with our approach.

Lesson: As the economy cycles and leadership changes, the organization will become more vulnerable to changes, some potentially harmful. To avoid getting swept along in the mad rush for survival, we must remain focused on our core values. They are the guideposts that have helped us weather tough times in the past and stay in business for over 110 years.

Your values are about who you are. They are our true north, or moral compass. Our values are why people have stuck with us through thick and thin. We will have lean times again, and it is our value system that will get us through them. During the most difficult times in our history, the Sundt values were never compromised. We may have been close to going out of business, but we knew this was too good a company to let fail and we could and would get through our difficulties.

Lesson: We had the courage to invest in our people by investing heavily in their training and development, as well as in technology enhancements that improve productivity and quality. This is not easy to do when you are almost broke, but we strongly believed it was the right thing to do to put us on a path to success. Even during salary freezes and layoffs, we never cut our training or technology budgets because we knew we needed them to be successful in the future. You can't just abandon your principles in tough times because, if you do, it is almost always analogous to digging the hole deeper a lot faster.

Lesson: Never forget the fundamentals of business that we have discussed in this book, especially discipline. The things we changed, such as strategic planning, training and development, technology investments, succession planning, and asset management, are things that *must* stay institutionalized and adhered to if you are going to be successful in the long-term.

Lesson: We found that you have to avoid focusing sometimes on the ends and pay attention to the means. For instance, we talked about how we learned from the Harvard balanced scorecard that while the end goal may be profits, you can't lose sight of how they are earned. It is the right people in the right roles, working with continually improved business processes and focused on the needs of the customer that drives profitability. It just does not happen any other way.

We are finding this to be true in other areas of the company such as business development. If you just focus on the end result of how much new work you

analysis (where is the money?) managing relationships, understanding the differentiators for the customer and delivering them, and so on.

Lesson: Change is inevitable, but the differentiator is how well the organization is at implementing change. We had to change a lot of things at Sundt just to survive, and one of the good things that resulted, particularly for a construction company, is that we developed a good capacity for change. That is a skill set that needs to be built upon and has a direct relationship with our ability to innovate and strategically plan, both of which, done well, will have a lot to do with Sundt's future success.

These lessons are already being taken to heart. We see it on a daily basis. There is a fresh, new, exciting pride among our people that could not be classified as arrogance. We have been extraordinarily successful during the last ten years. But this time, nobody is arrogant. This time our people are not sitting back, assuming the good times will roll on without their active involvement. We have engaged employees who are aligned with management's vision and what needs to be done to sustain our success into the future. Success has driven their desire to have more success.

Back in the introduction we said that we hope our turnaround story provides an institutional memory for our future leaders of how we did it and what things led to the decay so that they can avoid making the same mistakes again. As we write this book, the world is facing some of the most difficult economic times we've ever seen. It is times like these that reinforce the importance of ingraining each lesson and fundamental we have talked about into our (and your) company's corporate culture. When every single policy, principle, and value you have worked tirelessly to develop, build upon, and impart to your people is strenuously tested by a challenging business environment such as the one that all business leaders are facing now, the fruits of your efforts are quickly revealed. So far, we are fortunate that the edge of the abyss, which we once came so dangerously close to, is nowhere in sight. We can only hope that we have marked its path clearly for our future leaders with bold street signs so they never stumble blindly toward it again.

EPILOGUE

Richard's Final Words

My time at Sundt is coming to an end. I just hired my successor from one of the companies in the top 1 percent of our industry. As soon as he settled in and figured out what Sundt is all about, he said to me, "You were right, Richard. This is a special place." This is exactly what he was looking for in a job: a company to retire from.

Yet, who knows how this story would have played out if we hadn't had the Sundt reputation, the employee engagement, the Sundt family integrity, and the core values that really have been the glue that has defined and sustained the organization these last 120 years. It's easy to violate your principles when things are tough, but nobody at Sundt ever did. That option was never on the table.

Today's employee owners and leaders of Sundt have learned from our mistakes. They know that there is a delicate balance between not forgetting what got you this far, and doing the things that are going to take you even further. A company has to maintain discipline and never forget what happens when it does not.

The future of business, and the future of Sundt, is going to require finding a balance between focusing on our "day jobs," the tasks at hand, while getting more and more people within the organization looking toward the *next* thing. The top 1 percent of companies is figuring out the future while simultaneously succeeding in the present. The challenges for this next set of leaders are entirely different from the ones we faced. Our sole focus was on taking a company with severe financial trouble, turning it around, and creating an infrastructure to ensure that the mistakes of the past would never be repeated. The new leaders of Sundt have the freedom to take risks. If you have money, you can dare to do things that you can't do when you're struggling.

We have developed future leaders who have a foundation to soar higher and do things that Doug and I could never have imagined in the early '90s, because we were just struggling to stay afloat. The Sundt leaders of today have a much stronger foundation to take the company to new heights. The best days are ahead of us!

Doug's Final Words

As you read this book what becomes abundantly clear is that, as we have stated, it isn't about some silver bullet or magic potion; it's about discipline, focus, investing in your future by investing in your people and technology and creating an environment where people can learn grow and prosper; it's also about being a company that is making a difference in others' lives. We think we have accomplished this and we are telling this story because hopefully our experiences will help others do the same.

Wilson Sundt passed away from cancer four years ago; Bob Sundt is now eighty-five. The leaders who directly descended from our founder, M. M. Sundt, are no longer a part of the company, but they are not forgotten. Their core values still drive all of our decisions, and they always will.

I will be turning sixty-six in 2011 and will be leaving Sundt at the end of a long and very enjoyable career. I've learned that one of the worst things you can do in an organization is stay beyond when you're needed. I believe I was the right person for the times, but I'm not the best leader for the future. We now have the best talent we have had in my forty-five years here. There are future leaders across all divisions who will avoid the sins of our past. This book is about survival and the turnaround to sustainability, and these individuals know what it takes to sustain our success well into the future.

When I took over as CEO, I had the corporate history, a tremendous admiration for the Sundt family, a great concern about where we were, and a vision as to where we could go. This created a tremendous foundation for us to successfully move forward and take this company to the level of performance that all of its employee-owners deserved.

Now I'm passing the baton to Dave Crawford; I made the announcement two years ago to give Dave time to adjust to his new role. He is deeply committed to Sundt and well prepared, and I'm extremely confident he will be very successful in his new role.

The picture is different this time. There will be no last-minute drives from Tucson to Phoenix, or hastily drawn organization charts with crisscrossing lines. There will be no surprises. There will be no fear of succession because we are constantly training people to lead. The picture today is very different than it was on that fateful day in 1992 when Wilson came to my office to announce that I would become president of Sundt.

It's time for someone new to take the helm, and this time he is prepared to lead. And this time the ship is far from sinking. It is now full speed ahead.

About the Authors

J. Doug Pruitt is the Chairman and Chief Executive Officer of Sundt Construction Inc. which provides preconstruction and construction services through a variety of delivery methods such as construction management at risk, design-build, program management, and design-bid build. Sundt Construction has divisions to service projects in commercial and institutional buildings, highways, bridges, dams, light rail, multi-family and senior housing, telecommunications, wastewater and water treatment, utilities, mining and power.

Mr. Pruitt joined the Sundt family of companies in 1966. He has served as Executive Vice President and Manager of the Sundt's Building Division, Vice President/Manager of Construction Management Services and Chief Estimator of Sundt's Building Division. In May of 1992, assumed the position of President and Chief Operating Officer and in 1998 became Chairman and CEO.

He is the author of articles on concrete slipform mechanical cores for high-rise buildings and has chaired committees for the Associated General Contractors of America (AGC) producing brochures and videos on "Total Quality Management", "Partnering" and "Workforce Development."

Mr. Pruitt holds an AS in Civil Engineering from Oklahoma State University, and a BS in Business Administration from the University of Phoenix and a graduate of the Arizona State University Management Institute and the Stanford Executive Development Program.

About the Authors

Richard Condit is the Senior Vice President and Chief Administrative Officer of Sundt Construction Inc. which has an annual volume of $1 billion in preconstruction and construction services through a variety of delivery methods such as construction manager at risk, design-build, program management, build to suit and design-bid build. Sundt is a highly diversified general contractor with self performed capabilities in concrete, civil and utility construction processes.

Richard has responsibility for Human Resources, Strategic and Tactical Planning and Marketing and Business Development administration for the company. He joined the Sundt family of companies in 1993.

Richard holds a BS in Agricultural Education from the University of Arizona.

CPSIA information can be obtained
at www.ICGtesting.com
Printed in the USA
FFOW05n2114050314